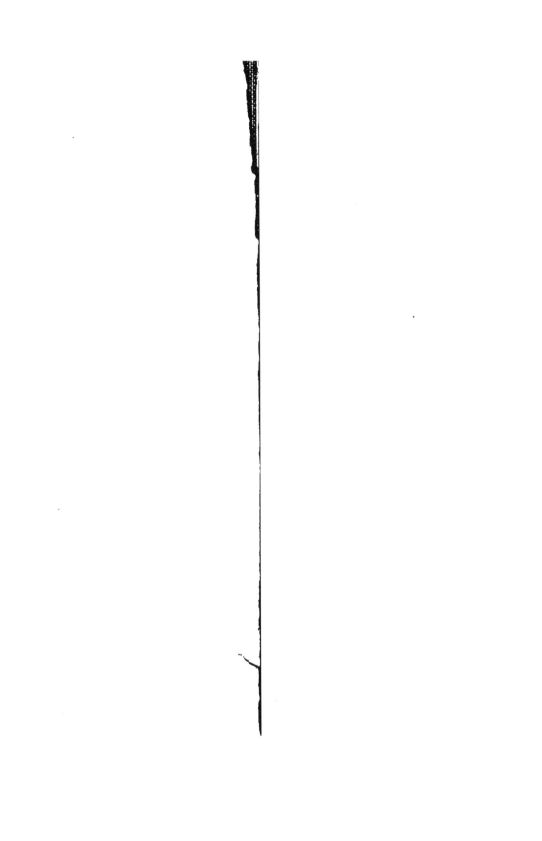

1

LETTERS OF
CHARLES DICKENS
TO
WILKIE COLLINS

EDITED BY

LAURENCE HUTTON

WITH PORTRAITS
AND FAC-SIMILES

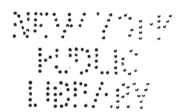

NEW YORK
HARPER & BROTHERS, PUBLISHERS
1892

LETTERS OF CHARLES DICKENS
TO WILKIE COLLINS.

WILLIAM WILKIE COLLINS was a man of
five or six and twenty when he first met
Charles Dickens, in 1851. He had spent two
years in study in Italy; four years as an ar-
ticled clerk to a city firm in the tea trade; he
had been a student of law in Lincoln's Inn;
he had written a biography of his father,
William Collins, R.A., who was a painter of
some repute; he had published his first novel,
Antonina, and he had determined to devote
himself thenceforth to a career of literature.

Charles Dickens at this period was near-
ly forty years of age. He had given to the
world the immortal *Pickwick, Oliver Twist,
Nicholas Nickleby, The Old Curiosity Shop,
Barnaby Rudge, The American Notes, Martin
Chuzzlewit, The Chimes, The Cricket on the*

I

Hearth, Dombey and Son, The Haunted Man,
and *David Copperfield;* and he had but re-
cently commenced the publication of the
weekly journal called *Household Words.* He
was the intimate of Thackeray, from whom he
was then not yet estranged, of Carlyle, Leigh
Hunt, Macaulay, Sydney Smith, Wilkie, Jerrold, Landor, Rogers, Longfellow, Washington Irving, Jeffrey, Turner, "Rugby" Arnold,
Leech, Lemon, and their peers; and he was
the recognized head of his guild in England.   The friendship and recognition of
such a man were of inestimable value to the
younger writer; and the intimacy then be-
gun, and cemented by the marriage of the
daughter of Dickens to the brother of Collins ten years later, continued unbroken until Dickens died in 1870.

The correspondence between them was
frequent and familiar.   Some portions of it
are to be found in *The Letters of Charles
Dickens*, edited by his sister-in-law and his
eldest daughter, and first published in 1880
as a supplement to Forster's *Life;* but a
large number of letters from Dickens to Collins were discovered after the death of Collins by his friend and literary executor, Mr.
A. P. Watt, who obtained from Miss Hogarth, the only remaining executor of Dick-

ens, permission to publish them. From these letters Miss Hogarth selected the following specimens as being quite as characteristic and fully as interesting as any she gave to the public in her own volume, and they have been printed here under her own supervision.

They not only show their writer as he was willing to show himself to the man whom he loved, but they give an excellent idea of his methods of collaboration with the man whom he had selected from all others as an active partner in certain of his creative works.

Why it is not possible to print herewith Collins's replies, Dickens himself fully explained in the following letter, which was written to Macready on the 1st of March, 1855, and which has already been printed by Miss Hogarth and Miss Dickens:

"Daily seeing improper uses made of confidential letters in the addressing of them to a public audience that has no business with them, I made, not long ago, a great fire in my field at Gad's Hill and burnt every letter I possessed. And now I destroy every letter I receive not on absolute business, and my mind is so far at ease."

That Macready should not have acted upon this hint and have destroyed this particular letter, with all the others which his friend at Gad's Hill had ever written to him, is proof enough of Macready's opinion of Dickens's charms as an epistolary correspondent. The reading world would have lost much if the biographers of Dickens, and the hundreds of men and women who were fortunate enough to have been his friends, had not appreciated the public as well as the private value of everything he put on paper, even in his private notes; and it is greatly to be regretted that he did not write letters to himself—like his own Mr. Toots— and preserve them all.

On the 10th of February, 1851, Dickens sent a note to Mr. W. H. Wills, his associate in conducting *Household Words*, asking him to take the part of a servant in the comedy of *Not so Bad as we Seem*, written by Bulwer for the Guild of Literature and Art, and played for the first time at Devonshire House in the month of May of the same year, by a company of very clever and very distinguished amateurs. " 'Mrs. Harris,' I says to her, 'be not alarmed; not reg'lar play-actors, hammertoors.' 'Thank 'Evens,' says Mrs. Harris, and bustiges into a flood of tears !"

Although Mr. Wills was actively interested in these entertainments, he does not seem ever to have appeared upon the stage; and Dickens was forced to seek a substitute, as the following letter will show. It was evidently given by its recipient, Augustus Egg, to its subject, and it was carefully cherished as long as Collins lived:

> Devonshire Terrace,
> Saturday Night, Eighth March, 1851.

MY DEAR EGG,—I think *you* told *me* that Mr. Wilkie Collins would be glad to play any part in Bulwer's Comedy; and I think *I* told *you* that I considered him a very desirable recruit. There is a Valet, called (as I remember) Smart—a small part, but, what there is of it, decidedly good; he opens the play—which I should be delighted to assign to him, and in which he would have an opportunity of dressing your humble servant, frothing some chocolate with an obsolete milling-machine that must be revived for the purpose, arranging the room, and dispatching other similar " business," dear to actors. Will you undertake to ask him if I shall cast him in this part? If yes, I will call him to the reading on Wednesday; have the pleasure of leaving my card for him (say where), and beg him to favor us with his company at dinner on Wednesday evening. I knew his father well, and should be very glad to know him.

Write me a word in answer, and believe me ever,   Faithfully yours,

CHARLES DICKENS.

The first letter from Dickens *to* Collins which has been preserved was ·dated two months later, and is here subjoined. The Duke was the Duke of Devonshire, who entertained the party at supper after· the first performance, and Mr. Ward was E. M. Ward, R.A., an early friend of Collins, who painted a portrait of Dickens in 1854.

No. 16, Wellington Street North, Strand,
Monday, Twelfth May, 1851.

MY DEAR COLLINS,—My only hesitation on the matter is this : I apprehend that the Duke, in his great generosity, intends to give a sort of supper to the whole party. I infer this from his so particularly desiring to know their number. *Now, I have already given him the list ;* and he is so delicate that he would not even ask Landseer without first asking me. Under these circumstances, I feel the introduction of a stranger like Mr. Ward's brother—Mr. Ward and his wife being already on the list—a kind of difficulty; but I do not like to refuse compliance with any wish of my faithful and attached valet, whom I greatly esteem. I therefore merely mention this and send him the order.

I have been here all day, and am covered with Sawdust.

> Faithfully yours always,
>> CHARLES DICKENS.

W. WILKIE COLLINS, Esquire.

So much has been written and said by men like Forster and Hans Christian Andersen, as well as by Dickens, about the famous theatrical representations in which Dickens was so prominent, that no additional word, even from an eye-witness, can be of any interest here. But the editor of the present papers, who was taken, when almost a child, by a thoughtful father to see one of these performances, will never forget the impression made upon him by the acting of the protagonist on that occasion. The Bill of the Play—which is here reproduced in

fac - simile — contains many great names,
which meant nothing then to the small boy
who waited so patiently that night for Dickens to appear, and Dickens himself meant
only David Copperfield. That small boy
had never heard of Mr. John Tenniel, of
Mr. Mark Lemon, of Mr. Augustus Egg, A.
R.A., of Mr. Frank Stone, of Mr. Peter Cun-
ningham, or of Mr. Wilkie Collins; but he
had read and reread *David Copperfield*, and
he looked upon it as a purely autobiograph-
ical and most delightful piece of work. He
knew Steerforth and Traddles better than
he knew many of his own school-mates;
he hated Uriah Heep and the Murdstones
more than he ever hated anybody else; he
loved Dora and Agnes better than he ever
expected, then, to love any woman but his
own mother; he had gone sobbing to his little bed when he heard of David's mother's
death, how " she was glad to lay her poor
head on her stupid, cross, old Peggotty's
arm; and she died like a child that had
gone to sleep." Peggotty, with her cheeks
and arms so hard and red that it was a wonder the birds didn't peck her in preference
to apples, was more real to him than the
Ann Hughes of his own nursery, whom no
bird would be disposed to peck under any

Philharmonic Hall, Liverpool.

Manager, Mr. CHARLES DICKENS, Tavistock House, Tavistock Square, in the County of Middlesex.

On FRIDAY EVENING, SEPTEMBER 3rd, 1862,

THE AMATEUR COMPANY

OF THE

GUILD OF LITERATURE & ART;

To encourage Life Assurance and other Provident Habits among Authors and Artists; to render such assistance to both as shall never compromise their independence; and to found a new Institution where honourable rest from arduous labour shall still be associated with the discharge of congenial duties;

WILL HAVE THE HONOR OF PRESENTING

(THIS BEING THEIR LAST NIGHT OF PERFORMANCE,)

THE PETITE COMEDY, IN TWO ACTS, OF

USED UP.

Sir Charles Coldstream, Bart...	...	Mr. CHARLES DICKENS,
Sir Adonis Leech,	...	Mr. COE
The Honorable Tom Saville,	...	Mr. JOHN TENNIEL,
Wurzel, (a Farmer)	...	Mr. F. W. TOPHAM,
John Ironbrace, (a Blacksmith)	...	Mr. MARK LEMON,
Mr. Fennel, (a Lawyer)	...	Mr. AUGUSTUS EGG, A.R.A.
James,	...	Mr. WILKIE COLLINS,

SCENERY.

Saloon in Sir Charles Coldstream's House. . . . . }
Distant View of the River, . . . } Painted by Mr. PITT.
Interior of an Old Farm House, . . . } Mr. STANFIELD, R.A.
} Mr. PITT.

Previous to the Play the Band will Perform an OVERTURE, composed expressly for this purpose, by Mr. C. COOTE, (Pianist to His Grace the Duke of Devonshire);

WHO WILL, ON THIS OCCASION, PRESIDE AT THE PIANOFORTE

To conclude with, (twenty-third time) an original Farce, in One Act, by Mr. CHARLES DICKENS
and Mr. MARK LEMON, entitled

MR. NIGHTINGALE'S DIARY.

Mr. NIGHTINGALE,	. . . . .	Mr. FRANK STONE, A.R.A.
Mr. GABBLEWIG, (of the Middle Temple)	. .	} Mr. CHARLES DICKENS.
CHARLEY BIT, (a Boots)	. . .	
Mr. POULTER, (a Pedestrian and Cold-Water Drinker)	.	
CAPTAIN BLOWER, (an Invalid)	. . .	
A RESPECTABLE FEMALE,	. . . .	
A DEAF SEXTON,	. . . .	
TIP, (Mr. GABBLEWIG'S Tiger)	. .	Mr. AUGUSTUS EGG, A.R.A.
CHRISTOPHER, (a Charity Boy)	. .	
SLAP, (professionally Mr. Flormiville—a Country Actor)		Mr. MARK LEMON.
Mr. TICKLE, (Inventor of the celebrated Compounds)		
A VIRTUOUS YOUNG PERSON IN THE CONFIDENCE OF "MARIA		Mr. WILKIE COLLINS.
LITHERS, (Landlord of the "Water Lily")	. .	Miss FANNY YOUNG.
ROSINA,	. . . .	Mrs. COE.
SUSAN,	. . . .	

The Proscenium by Mr. CRACE. The Theatre constructed by Mr. SLOMAN, Machinist of the Royal Lyceum Theatre.
The Properties and Appointments by Mr. G. FOSTER. The Costumes by Messrs. NATHAN, of Titchborne Street.
Perruquier, Mr. WILSON. Prompter, Mr. COE.

☞ THE WHOLE PRODUCED UNDER THE DIRECTION OF MR CHARLES DICKENS.

The Local Arrangements under the superintendence of Mr. William Sudlow.

Doors open at Six o Clock. To commence at exactly Seven o'clock; when the whole of the audience are particularly recommended to be seated.
Tickets to be had at the Offices of the Philharmonic Society; Exchange Court. Stalls (in the Body of the Hall and Room, 7s. 6d.;
Gallery Stalls, 5s. 6d.; Gallery Seats, 2s. 6d.

ENTRANCE TO ALL PARTS OF THE HALL FROM HOPE STREET.

A. IRELAND AND CO., PRINTERS, PALL MALL, MARKET STREET, MANCHESTER.

consideration; and although he had just made the grand tour for the first time, his only interest in the cathedral of St. Paul in London lay in the fact that it was pictured, with a pink dome, on the sliding lid of Peg-gotty's work-box. To see this grown-up David Copperfield in the flesh, doing all sorts of ridiculous things in the farce of *Mr. Nightingale's Diary;* to feel that, perhaps, he had a letter at that very moment in his pocket from the real Micawber; and that the actual Agnes was in the wings waiting to go home with him when the play was over, was to this particular little boy the greatest treat of his young life. And he has never ceased to thank the considerate father for the blessed memory of that wonderful night in Liverpool so many years ago.

That there existed a strong feeling of good-fellowship between Dickens and Collins from the very beginning of their acquaintance is indicated by the affectionate tone of the numerous letters which passed between them.

Lithers was the name of a character taken by Collins in one of the farcical afterpieces played by the company of amateurs, and Lord Wilmot was Dickens's part in *Not so Bad as we Seem.* Dickens was at work upon

Bleak House when he wrote to Collins from Boulogne, in June, 1853; and when that story was finished, in October, they started out, together with Augustus Egg, upon an excursion through parts of Switzerland and Italy; Egg being the Colonel alluded to as invited to "assist in scattering the family dinner" in April, 1854. The National Sparkler was one of the many names given to Dickens by himself. *Basil, a Story of Modern Life*, published in 1852, was Collins's first marked success as a writer of fiction, and Dickens alludes to it more than once in his letters to its author.

The occasional foot-notes signed "W. W. C." are in the handwriting of Collins. The parentheses in square brackets have been, on all occasions, added by the Editor.

Tavistock House,
Twenty-third December, 1852.

MY DEAR COLLINS,—I am suddenly laid by the heels in consequence of Wills having gone blind without any notice—I hope and believe from mere temporary inflammation. This obliges me to be at the office all day to-day, and to resume my attendance there to-morrow. But if you will come there to-

morrow afternoon — say at about three
o'clock—I think we may forage pleasantly
for a dinner in the City,. and then go and
look at Christmas Eve in Whitechapel, which
is always a curious thing.

The end of this letter (cut off for an autograph-
hunter) simply mentioned the receipt of an odd
letter from a namesake of mine inquiring for my
address.—W. W. C.

Tavistock House,
Tuesday, January Eighteenth, 1853.

MY DEAR COLLINS,—If you should be disposed to revel in the glories of the eccentric
British Drayma, on Saturday evening, I am
the man to join in so great a movement.
My money is to be heard of at the Bar of
the Household Words at five o'clock on
that afternoon.

Gin Punch is also to be heard of at the
Family Arms, Tavistock, on Sunday next at
five, when the National Sparkler will be
prepared to give Lithers a bellyful if he
means anything but Bounce.

I have been thinking of the Italian proj-
ect, and reducing the time to two months
—from the 20th October to the 20th De-

cember—see the way to a trip that shall really not exclude any foremost place, and be reasonable too.   Details when we meet.

Ever faithfully,   C. D.

Chateau des Moulineaux,
Rue Beaurepaire, Boulogne,
Friday, Twenty-fourth June, 1853.

MY DEAR COLLINS,—I hope you are as well as I am, and have as completely shaken off all your ailings.   And I hope, too, that you are disposed for a long visit here.   We are established in a doll's country house of many rooms in a delightful garden.   If you have · anything to do, this is the place to do it in.   And if you have nothing to do, this is also the place to do it in to perfection.

You shall have a Pavilion room in the garden, with a delicious view, where you may write no end of Basils.   You shall get up your Italian as I raise the fallen fortunes (at present sorely depressed) of mine.   You shall live, with a delicate English graft upon the best French manner, and learn to get up early in the morning again.   In short, you shall be thoroughly prepared, during the whole summer season, for those great travels that are to come off anon.

Do turn your thoughts this way, coming by South Eastern *Tidal Train* (there is a separate list for that train, the time changing every day as the tide varies), you come in five hours. No passport wanted. Mrs. Dickens and her sister send their kind regards, and beg me to say how glad they will be to see you.

W. WILKIE COLLINS, Esquire.

Our united remembrances to your mother and brother.

Boulogne, Thirtieth June, 1853.
Thursday.

MY DEAR COLLINS,—I am very sorry indeed to hear so bad an account of your illness, and had no idea it had been so severe. I can't help writing (though most unnecessarily I hope) to say that you can't get well too soon; and that 'I warrant the pure air, regular hours, and perfect repose of this place to bring you round triumphantly. You have only, when you are sufficiently restored, to defy the D—octor and all his works, to write me a line naming your day and hour.

My friend *Lord Wilmot* will then be found at the Custom House.

Ward's account of me was the true one. I was thoroughly disabled—in a week—and doubt if you would have known me. But I recovered with surprising quickness, positively insisting on coming here, against all advice but [Dr.] Elliotson's — and got to work next day but one as if nothing had happened.

And what was the matter with me? Sir —I find this reads like Dr. Johnson directly —Sir, it was an old, afflicted

KIDNEY,

once the torment of my childhood, in which I took cold.

Signature cut off for autograph-hunters.—W. C.

Tavistock House, Friday Night,
Twenty-fourth February, 1854.

MY DEAR COLLINS,—Sitting reading to-night, it comes into my head to say that if you look into Montaigne's *Journey into Italy* (not much known now, I think, except to readers), you will find some passages that would be curious for extract. They are

very well translated into a sounding kind of
old English in Hazlitt's translation of Montaigne.

If you are disengaged next Saturday,
March the 4th, and it should be a fine day,
what do you say to making it the occasion
for our Rochester trip?

Faithfully yours always,   C. D.

W. WILKIE COLLINS, Esquire.

Tavistock House, Monday,
Twenty-fourth April, 1854.

MY DEAR COLLINS,—I met the Colonel
at the Water Colors on Saturday, and asked
him if he would assist in scattering the family dinner next Sunday at half past 5, as
usual.   Will you join us, Sir?

Beaucourt's house above the Moulineaux,
on the top of the hill—free and windy—not
so bijou-ish, but larger rooms, and possess-
ing a back gate and a field, secured by the
undersigned contracting party from the middle of June to the middle of October.   I
hope you will write the third volume of
"that" book there.

[Chauncey Hare] Townshend coming to

town on the 12th of May.   Pray Heaven he
may not have another choral birthday, and
another frolicultural * cauliflower.

Ever faithfully,   C. D.

* I think this word a bold one.   It is intended
for floricultural.—C. D.

Tavistock House,
Sixth June, 1854.

MY DEAR COLLINS :

Form of trip appointment, in compliance with Act of Parliament. Victoria, cap. 7, sec. 304.		
	Day,	Thursday.
	Hour,	Quarter past 11 A.M.
	Place,	Dover Terminus, London Bridge.
	Destination,	Tunbridge Wells.
	Description of Railway Qualification, Return Ticket.	
	(Signed)	CHARLES DICKENS.
	Entd.	

Tavistock House,
Seventh June, 1854.

MY DEAR COLLINS,—Mark has got something in his foot—which is not Gout, of

course, though it has a family likeness to that disorder — which he thinks will disable him to-morrow. Under these circumstances, and as this inclement season of summer has set in with so much severity, I think it may be best to postpone our expedition. Will you take a stroll on Hampstead Heath, and dine here on Sunday instead? And if yes, will you be here at 2?

Ever faithfully, C. D.

On the 22d of July, 1854, Dickens wrote to Miss Hogarth, as quoted in *The Letters:*

"Neither you nor Catherine [Mrs. Dickens] did justice to Collins's book [*Hide and Seek*]. I think it far away the cleverest novel I have ever seen written by a new hand. It is in some respects masterly. Valentine Blyth is as original, and as well done, as anything can be. The scene where he shows his pictures is full of an admirable humor. Old Mat is admirably done. In short, I call it a very remarkable book, and have been very much surprised by its great merit."

2

Miss Hogarth is unable to explain the allusion to the "Cowell facts," in the letter
of December 17, 1854. The "Mark" referred to in this and subsequent letters was
Mark Lemon, editor of *Punch*.

Tavistock House,
Sunday, Seventeenth December, 1854.

MY DEAR COLLINS,—Many thanks for
your note. As I rode home in the hansom,
that Gravesend night, one or two doubts
arose in my mind respecting the Cowell
facts; and before breakfast on the following morning I wrote to Mark, begging him
to say nothing to Jerrold from me until I
should have satisfied my mind. I am so
sorry at heart for the working-people when
they get into trouble, and have their wretched arena chalked out for them with such extraordinary complacency by small political
economists, that I have a natural impulse
upon me, almost always, to come to the rescue—even of people I detest, if I believe
them to have been true to these poor men.

I am away to Reading to read the *Carol*,
and to Sherborne, and, after Christmas Day,
to Bradford, in Yorkshire. The thirtieth

will conclude my public appearances for the present season, and then I hope we shall have some Christmas diversions here. I have got the children's play into shape, so far as the Text goes (it is an adaptation of *Fortunio*), but it has not been " on the stage " yet. Mark is going to do the Dragon—with a practicable head and tail.

Ever yours,   .C. D.

On the 6th of January, 1855, at Tavistock House, Dickens, Collins, and Lemon played in *The Fairy Extravaganza of Fortunio and his Seven Gifted Sons*, by Mr. Planché, the rest of the cast comprising the Dickens children and some of their juvenile friends. " They are all agog now," Dickens wrote a few days before, " about a great fairy play which is to come off here next Monday. The house is full of spangles, gas, Jews, theatrical tailors, and pantomime carpenters."

Tavistock House,
Christmas Eve, 1854.

MY DEAR COLLINS,— Here is a Part in *Fortunio*—dozen words—but great Pantomime opportunities—which requires a first-rate old stager to devour Property Loaves.

Will you join the joke and do it? Gobbler, one of the seven gifted servants, is the Being "to let." There is an eligible opportunity of making up dreadfully greedy.

I am going to read the piece to the children next Tuesday, at half past 2. We shall rehearse it at the same hour every day in the following week—dress rehearsal on Saturday night, the 6th ; night of performance, Monday, the 8th.

I am just come back from Reading and Sherborne, and go to Bradford on Wednesday morning, returning next day.

If you should chance to be disengaged to-day, here we are—Pork, with sage and inions, at half past 5.   - Ever faithfully,   C. D.

W. WILKIE COLLINS, Esquire.

Tavistock House,
Sunday, Fourth March, 1855.

MY DEAR COLLINS,—I have to report another failure on the part of our friend " Williams " last night. He so confounded an enlightened British audience at the Standard Theatre on the subject of *Antony and Cleopatra* that I clearly saw them wondering, towards the end of the Fourth Act, when the play was going to begin.

A man much heavier than Mark (in the actual scale, I mean), and about twenty years older, played Cæsar. When he came on with a map of London — pretending it was a scroll and making believe to read it—and said, "He calls me Boy"—a howl of derision arose from the audience which you probably heard in the Dark, without knowing what occasioned it. All the smaller characters, having their speeches much upon their minds, came in and let them off without the slightest reference to cues. And Miss Glyn, in some entirely new conception of her art, "read" her part like a Patter song—several lines on end with the rapidity of Charles Mathews, and then one very long word. It was very brightly and creditably got up, but (as I have said) "Williams" did not carry the audience, and I don't think the Sixty Pounds a week will be got back by the Manager.

You will have the goodness to picture me to yourself—alone—in profound solitude—in an abyss of despair—ensconced in a small

Managerial Private Box in the very centre of the House — frightfully sleepy (I had a dirty steak in the City first, and I think they must have put Laudanum into the Harvey's sauce), and played at, point-blank, by the entire strength of the company. The horrors in which I constantly woke up, and found myself detected, you will imagine. The gentle Glyn, on being called for, heaved her snowy bosom straight at me, and the box-keeper informed me that the Manager who brought her on would " have the honor of stepping round directly." I sneaked away in the most craven and dastardly manner, and made an utterly false representation that I was coming back again.

If you will give me one glass of hot gin-and-water on Thursday or Friday evening, I will come up about 8 ( )* o'clock with a cigar in my pocket and inspect the Hospital. I am afraid this relaxing weather will tell a little faintly on your medicine, but I hope you will soon begin to see land beyond the Hunterian Ocean.

* ( ) Intended for "eight."—C. D.

I have been writing and planning and making notes over an immense number of little bits of paper—and I never can write legibly under such circumstances.

Always cordially yours,   C. D.

W. WILKIE COLLINS, Esquire.

Sister Rose, a story in four parts, by Collins, was printed in *Household Words*, in April and May, 1855.   Mr. Pigott is Mr. Edward Pigott, an intimate friend of Collins, and the present " Licenser of Plays " in the Lord Chamberlain's office.   He was in the cast of *The Frozen Deep*, produced by Dickens and Collins two years later.

Tavistock House,
Monday, Nineteenth March, 1855.

MY DEAR COLLINS,—I have read the two first portions of *Sister Rose* with the very greatest pleasure.   An excellent story, charmingly written, and shewing everywhere an amount of pains and study in respect of the art of doing such things that I see mighty seldom.

If I be right in supposing that the brother and sister are concealing the husband's

mother, then will you look at the closing
scene of the second part again, and consider whether you cannot make the idica-
tion of that circumstance a little more ob-
scure—or, at all events, a little less emphatic:
as by Rose's only asking her brother once
for leave to tell her husband, or some slight
alteration of that kind? The best way I
know of strengthening the interest and hit-
ting this point would be the introduction or
mention, in the first instance, *of some one
other person* who *might* (in the reader's divided thoughts) be the concealed person,
and of whom the husband might have a
latent dislike or jealousy — as a friend of
the brother's. But this might involve too
great a change.

If, on the other hand, it be not the mother
who is visited, then it is clear that you have
altogether succeeded as it stands, and have
entirely misled me.

How are you getting on? Shall you be
up to a day at Ashford to-morrow week? I
shall be able to frank you down and up the
Railway on the solemn occasion. Mark
(whose face is at present enormous) is go-

ing, and Wills will tell us the story of the Bo'sen, whose artful chaff, in that sparkling dialogue, played the Devil with T. Cooke.

Talking of which feat, I wish you could have seen your servant last Wednesday beleaguer the Literary Fund. They got so bothered and bewildered that I expected to see them all fade away under the table; and the outsiders laughed so irreverently whenever I poked up the chairman that it was quite a facetious business. Virtually, I consider the thing done. You may believe that I am not about to let go, and the effect has far and far exceeded my expectations already. Mark is full of the subject and will tell you all about it. . . .

What is Mr. Pigott's address? I want to leave a card for him.

Ever faithfully,   C. D.

Tavistock House,
Saturday, Twenty-fourth March, 1855.

MY DEAR COLLINS,—I am charmed to hear of the great improvement, and really hope now that you are beginning to see land.

The train (an express one) leaves London Bridge Station on Tuesday at half past 11 in the forenoon. Fire and comfort are ordered to be in readiness at the Inn at Ashford. We shall have to return at half past 2 in the morning—getting to town before 5 —but the interval between the Reading and the Mails will be spent by what would be called in a popular musical entertainment " the flick o' our ain firesides "—which reminds me to observe that I am dead sick of the Scottish tongue in all its moods and tenses.

You have guessed right! The best of it was that she [Mrs. Gaskell] wrote to Wills, saying she must particularly stipulate not to have her proofs touched, "even by Mr. Dickens." That immortal creature had gone over the proofs [*North and South*] with great pains—had of course taken out the stiflings —hard-plungings, lungeings, and other convulsions—and had also taken out her weakenings and damagings of her own effects. "Very well," said the gifted Man, "she shall have her own way. But after it's published shew her this Proof, and ask her to consider whether her story would have been the better or the worse for it."

When you see Millais, tell him that if he would like a quotation for his fireman picture there is a very suitable and appropriate one to be got from Gay's *Trivia*. . . .

Ever yours,
CHARLES DICKENS.

I dined with an old General yesterday, who went perfectly mad at dinner about the *Times*—exudations taking place from his mouth while he denied all its statements, that were partly foam, and partly turbot with white sauce. He persisted, likewise, in speaking of that Journal as " Him."

Tavistock House,
Wednesday, Fourth April, 1855.

MY DEAR COLLINS,—I have read the article in the *Leader* on Napoleon's reception in England with great pleasure and entire concurrence. I think it is forcible and just, and yet states the real case with great moderation. Not knowing of it, I had been speaking to its author on that very subject in the Pit of the Olympic on Saturday night.

And, by-the-bye, as the Devil would have it (for I assume that he is always up to something, and that everything is his fault— I being, as you know, evangelical), I mislaid your letter with Mr. Pigott's address in it, and "didn't like" to ask him for it. Do, like an amiable, corroded hermit, send me that piece of information again.

I hope the medical authorities will not— as I may say—cut your nose off to be revenged on your face. You might want it at some future time. It is but natural that the Doctor should þe irritated by so much opposition—still, isn't the offending feature in some sort a man and a brother?

The Pantomine was amazingly good, and it really was a comfortable thing to see all conventional dignity so outrageously set at naught. It was astonishingly well done, and extremely funny. Not a man in it who wasn't quite as good as the Humbugs who pass their lives in doing nothing else. I observed at the Fund Dinner that the actors are in the same condition about it as they were when we played. Idiots!

May the Spring advance with rosy foot,

and the voice of the Turtle be shortly heard in the land.   Ever faithfully,   C. D.

Tavistock House,
Sunday, Fifteenth April, 1855.

MY DEAR COLLINS,—Hurrah!

I shall be charmed to see you once more in a Normal state, and propose Friday next for our meeting at the Garrick, at a quarter before 5. We will then proceed to the Ship and Turtle.

I fell foul of Wills yesterday, for that in "dealing with" the second part of your story [*Sister Rose*] he had not (in two places) "indoctrinated" the Printer with the change of name. He explained to me that on the whole, and calmly regarding all the facts from a politico-economical point of view, it was a more triumphant thing to have two mistakes than none—and, indeed, that, philosophically considered, this was rather the object and province of a periodical.

Faithfully always,   C. D.

Collins was at this time a constant contributor to *Household Words*, and his *After*

Dark (1856) and *Dead Secret* (1857) originally appeared in that periodical. The great success of *Fortunio* inspired Mr. Crummles, the
Manager—a name given by Dickens to himself—to attempt the production of a more
serious play, and led to the writing by Collins of *The Light-house*, a drama which was
afterwards seen upon the public boards of
the London Olympic. On May 20 Dickens
wrote to Clarkson Stanfield:

" I have a little lark in contemplation, if
you will help it to fly. Collins has done a
melodrama (a regular old style melodrama),
in which there is a very good notion. I am
going to act in it, as an experiment, in the
children's theatre here [Tavistock House].
I, Mark, Collins, Egg, and my daughter Mary,
the whole *dram. pers.* . . . . Now there is only
one scene in the piece, and that, my tarry
lad, is the inside of a light-house. Will you
come and paint it?"

Nothing has been recorded concerning
the acting of the author; but Carlyle, who
was present as a first-nighter, compared
Dickens's wild picturesqueness in the old
light-house keeper to the famous ·figure in

Nicholas Poussin's bacchanalian dance in the National Gallery. Mr. Stanfield's original sketch for the scene of the Eddystone Light-house, which hung in the hall at Gad's Hill until Dickens died, was afterwards sold for a thousand guineas.

The ticket referred to in the letter of June 24, 1855, was a card of admission to a meeting of "The Administrative Reform League," held in Drury Lane Theatre, at which Dickens made an effective speech. Colonel Waugh was at that time living in Campden House, Church Street, Kensington, a fine old mansion since destroyed by fire. It contained a private theatre, in which the Company of Amateurs gave several performances.

Tavistock House,
Friday, Eleventh May, 1855.

MY DEAR COLLINS,—I will read the play referring to the Light-house with great pleasure if you will send it to me—of course will at any time, with cordial readiness and unaffected interest, do any such thing. . . .

I hope to make Folkestone the country quarters for this Autumn. At the end of October I have an idea of removing the caravan to Paris for six months. I wish you would come over too, and take a Bedroom hard by us. It strikes me that a good deal might be done for *Household Words* on that side of the water.

But we shall have plenty of leisure to talk about this at Folkestone.

I have seen nothing of —— since he disarranged the whole metropolitan supply of gas. I have a general idea that he must have been upside down ever since, in some corner—like the groom to whom the sultan's daughter was to have been sacrificed.. He was indeed Great and Grand. I went about the streets all next day, laughing like a Pantomime mask. I never did see anything so ridiculous.

The restless condition in which I wander up and down my room with the first page of my new book [*Little Dorrit*] before me defies all description. I feel as if nothing would do me the least good but setting up a Balloon. It might be inflated in the garden in front—but I am afraid of its scarcely clearing those little houses.

Ever faithfully,   C. D.

Tavistock House,
Thursday, Twenty-first May, 1855.

MY DEAR COLLINS,—Lemon assures me that the Parts and Prompt book are to arrive to-day. Why they have not been here two days I cannot for the life of me make out. In case they *do* come, there is a good deal in the way of clearing the ground that you and I may do before the first Rehearsal. Therefore, will you come and dine at 6 to-morrow (Friday) and give the evening to it?

Faithfully ever,   C. D.

Tavistock House,
Saturday Morning, June Ninth, 1855.

MY DEAR COLLINS,—I have had a communication from Stanfield since we parted last night, to the effect that he must have the Stage entirely to himself and his men on Thursday Night. I therefore write round to all the company, to remind them that Monday is virtually our last Rehearsal, and that we shall probably have to do your Play twice on that precious occasion.

Ever heartily yours,   C. D.

3

Tavistock House.
Sunday, Twenty-fourth June, 1855.

MY DEAR COLLINS,—I am delighted that
I have this one ticket to spare out of six
that I got for Home.   If you will be at the
principal door in Brydges Street a little before a quarter to 7, and will there meet my
people as they come up, and go in with them,
you will find your place secured.   The Sec-
retary writes me that it is necessary to be
early, to avoid calling attention to this fact,
as other places are *not* secured.

I am rather flustered about the thing just
now, not knowing their ways, or what kind
of audience they are, or how they go on at
all.   But I'll try them, and the best can do
no more.

I have broached a move Kensingtonwards,
for changing their arrangements altogether
—dropping the Farce—putting their piece
second—and playing *The Light-house* (Original cast and Scenery) first.   I don't know
whether anything may come of it, but I
thought it well to make a discreet point that
way.   This for the present entirely between
ourselves.

Will you tell your brother, with my regards, that I write to Townshend by to-morrow morning's mail? I am not *quite* sure
where he is.   Ever yours,   C. D.

Tavistock House,
Sunday, Eighth July, 1855.

MY DEAR COLLINS,—I don't know whether
you may have heard from [Benjamin] Webster, or whether the impression I derived
from Mark's manner on Friday may be altogether correct. But it strongly occurred
to me that Webster was going to decline the
Play, and that he really has worried himself
into a fear of playing Aaron.

Now, when I got this into my head—
which was during the Rehearsal—I considered two things—firstly, how we could best
put about the success of the piece more
widely and extensively even than it has yet
reached, and, secondly, how you could be
best assured against a bad production of it
hereafter, or no production of it. I thought
I saw, immediately, that the point would be
to have this representation noticed in the
Newspapers. So I waited until the Re-

hearsal was over and we had profoundly as-
tonished the family, and then asked Colonel
Waugh what he thought of sending some
cards for Tuesday to the papers.   He highly approved, and yesterday morning direct-
ed Mitchell to send to all the morning papers, and to some of the weekly ones — a
dozen in the whole.

I dined at Lord John's [Russell] yesterday (where Meyerbeer was, and said to me
after dinner, "Ah, mon ami illustre !   Que
c'est noble de vous entendre parler d'haute
voix morale, à la table d'un Ministre !"—for
I gave them a little bit of truth about Sunday, that was like bringing a Sebastopol bat-
tery among the polite company)—I say, after this long parenthesis, I dined at Lord
John's, and found great interest and talk
about the Play, and about what everybody
who had been here had said of it.   And I
was confirmed in my decision that the thing
for you was the Invitation to the papers.
Hence I write to tell you what I have done.

I dine at home at half past 5, if you are
disengaged, and shall be at home all the
evening.   Ever faithfully,   C. D.

For the Christmas number of *Household Words* in 1855 Dickens and Collins wrote, together, *The Holly Tree*, Dickens contributing *Myself*, *Boots*, and *The Bill* according to the bibliography contained in Forster's *Life*.

Hotel des Bains, Boulogne,
Sunday, Fourteenth October, 1855.

MY DEAR COLLINS,—Behold me in our old quarters, which are as comfortable as usual. Crossed yesterday. Fine overhead, but heaving and surging sea. The Plorn [a nickname given to his youngest son, Edward Bulwer Lytton Dickens] wonderfully sick, but wonderfully good—making no complaint whatever—feeling the unreasonableness and hopelessness of the Ocean. . . .

The Ostler [in *The Holly Tree*] shall be yours, and I think the sketch involves an extremely good and startling idea. I am not, however, sure but that it trails off in the sudden disappearance of the woman without any result or explanation, and that some such thing may not be wanted for the purpose—unless her never being heard of any more could be so very strikingly described as to supply the place of other cul-

mination to the story.   Will you consider
that point again ?

I purpose being in town on the 13th of
November.   It is our Audit Day.   Perhaps
you will dine at the office at half past 5 ?

Kindest regards from all.

                    Ever faithfully yours,
                              CHARLES DICKENS.

W. WILKIE COLLINS, Esquire.

Paris, 49 Avenue des Champs Elysées,
Wednesday, Twelfth December, 1855.

MY DEAR COLLINS,—. . . I leave here for
town on Saturday, but shall have to start
for Peterborough on Monday morning.   If
you are free on Wednesday (when I shall
return from that reading), and will meet me
at the *Household Words* office at half past 5,
I shall be happy to start on any Haroun Al-
raschid expedition.

Think of my going down to Sheffield on
Friday, to read there—in the bitter winter—
with journey back to Paris before me.

I thought your Christmas Story [*The Ostler*] *immensely improved* in the working out.
The botheration of that No. has been pro-

digious. The general matter was so disappointing, and so impossible to be fitted together or got into the frame, that after I had done the *Guest* and the *Bill*, and thought myself free for a little *Dorrit* again, I had to go back once more (feeling the thing too weak), and do the *Boots*. Look at said *Boots;* because I think it's an odd idea, and gets something of the effect of a Fairy Story out of the most unlikely materials. . . .

Every Frenchman who can write a begging letter writes one, and leaves it for this apartment. He first of all buys any literary composition printed in quarto on tea-paper with a limp cover, scrawls upon it " Hommage à Charles Dickens, l'illustre Romancier " — encloses the whole in a dirty envelope, reeking with tobacco smoke — and prowls, assassin-like, for days, in a big cloak and an enormous *cachenez* like a counterpane, about the scraper of an outer door.

Ever faithfully,   C. D.

Reply as to Wednesday, in note to Tavistock House for receipt there on Sunday.

49 Champs Elysées,
Thirtieth January, 1856, Wednesday.

MY DEAR COLLINS,—I hope you are "out of the wood, and holloaing."

I purpose coming to town either on Monday or Tuesday night, and returning (if convenient to you), on the following Sunday or Monday. I will write to you as soon as I arrive, and arrange for our devoting an early evening (I should like Wednesday next) to letting our united observation with extended view "survey mankind from China to Peru." On second thoughts, shall we appoint Wednesday now? Unless I hear from you to the contrary, I will expect you at *Household Words* at 5 that day.

Ever faithfully (working hard),   C. D.

49 Champs Elysées, Paris,
Tuesday, Twelfth February, 1856.

MY DEAR COLLINS,—I am delighted to receive your letter — which is just come to hand—and heartily congratulate you upon it. I have no doubt you will soon appear. I would recommend you, unless the Boulogne Boat serves to a marvel, to come by the Calais route—the day mail. Because in the winter there are no special trains on that Boulogne line in France, and waiting at Boulogne is a bore. The Pavilion is all ready, and is a wonder. Upon my word, it is the snuggest oddity I ever saw—the lookout from it the most wonderful in the world. . . .

We had a pleasant trip, and the best dinner at the " Bang " [Hôtel des Bains], Boulogne, I ever sat down to.

` So, looking out for your next letter "advising self " of your coming,

Ever faithfully,   C. D.

49 Champs Elysées, Paris.
Sunday, Twenty-fourth February, 1856.

MY DEAR COLLINS,—The Post still coming in to-day without any intelligence from you, I am getting quite uneasy. From day to day I have hoped to hear of your recovery, and have forborne to write, lest I should unintentionally make the time seem longer to you. But I am now so very anxious to know how you are that I cannot hold my hand any longer. So pray let me know

by return.   And if you should unhappily be
too unwell to write yourself, pray get your
brother to represent you.

I cannot tell you how unfortunate I feel
this to be, or how disconsolately I look at
the uninhabited Pavilion.

Ever faithfully,   C. D.

Dickens spent the winter of 1855–56, or
the greater part of it, in Paris.   On the
26th of March he wrote to Macready: "You
will find us in the queerest of little rooms
all alone, except that the son of Collins,
the painter (who writes a good deal in
Household Words) dines with us every day."
Here they planned *The Wreck of the Golden
Mary*, which appeared in *Household Words*
the following Christmas, and here they conceived the idea of *The Frozen Deep*, a drama
written by Collins for performance at Tavistock House.

The version of *As You Like It* which
amused Dickens and Macready so much
was by Georges Sand, who is, unquestionably, the "she" mentioned by Dickens as
knowing "just nothing at all about it."   It
is strange that the fact that Madame Dude-
vant introduces Shakespeare as one of the

characters in his own comedy did not strike Dickens as worthy of remark.

The Poole mentioned in the letter of April 13th, and later throughout the correspondence, was John Poole, the dramatist, whom Dickens helped in many ways, and who, at Dickens's urgent request, was placed on the Civil List as a pensioner in 1850. M. Forgues was at that time (1856) editor of the *Revue des Deux Mondes*, for whom Dickens, at Collins's request, wrote a fragment of autobiography.

Champs Elysées,
Sunday, April Thirteenth, 1856.

MY DEAR COLLINS,—We checked you off at the various points of your journey all day, but never dreamed of the half gale. You must have had an abominable passage with that convivial club. My soul sickens at the thought of it; and the smell seized hold of the bridge of my nose exactly half-way up, and won't let it go again.

Your portress duly appeared with the small account and your note. I paid her immediately, of course, and she departed rejoicing. The Pavilion looks very desolate, and nobody has taken it as yet. Macready left us at 7 yesterday morning, and I afterwards took a long country walk to get into train for work. It was a noble spring day, and the air most delightful. But I found the evening sufficiently dull, and indeed we all miss you very much. . . .

Macready went on Friday to the Rehearsal of *Comme il vous plaira* [*As You Like It*], which was produced last night. His account of it was absolutely stunning. The speech of the Seven Ages delivered as a light comedy joke; Jacques at the Court of the Reigning Duke instead of the banished one, and winding up the thing by *marrying Celia!* Everything as wide of Shakespeare as possible, and confirming my previous impression that she knew just nothing at all about it. She was to have been here on Friday evening, but had "la migraine" (of which I think you have heard before); but Regnier said, as to the piece, "La pièce. Il n'y a point de pièce," tapped his forehead with great violence, and threw whatever liquid came out into the air, as an offering to the offended gods. Girardin

said, "Qu'il l'avait trouvé à la répétition très
intéressante, très intéressante, très intéressante !"—and said nothing more the whole
evening. I dine at another of his prodigious
banquets to-morrow.

I am very anxious to know what your
Doctor says. If he should fail to set you up
by the 3d or 4th of May for me I shall consider him a Humbug. It occurs to me to
mention that if you don't get settled in May,
the Hogarths will then leave Tavistock
House to me and Charley, and you know
how easily and amply it can accommodate
you. Pray don't forget that it is available
for your quarters. There will be two or
three large airy bedrooms with nobody to
occupy them, and the range of the whole
sheeted house besides. The Pavilion of
the Moulineaux I shall, of course, reserve
for your summer occupation and work.
Talking of which latter, I am reminded to
say that the Scotch Housekeeper is secured.

You know exactly where I am sitting,
what I am seeing, what I am hearing, what
is going on around me in every way. I have
not a scrap of news, except that Poole, at

the Français, complained bitterly to Macready of your humble servant's neglect,
which, considering that he would unquestionably be in some remote English work-
house but for me, I think characteristic.
Macready's reply to him appears to have
been : " Er—really—er—no Poole :—er—
must excuse me—host—um—friend—er—
great affection—um—cannot permit—er—
must therefore distinctly beg. . . ."

All unite in kindest regard and best wishes for your speedily coming all right again.

Ever faithfully,

CHARLES DICKENS.

I enclose a letter from Forgues. The book
of the *Light-house* accompanies it, which I
will bring with me.

P.P.S. — According to a highly illegible
note I have from Forgues, it would seem
that I ought to send you the book with
some idea of your sending it back to me
to send to him. The little Lemons therefore shall bring the book with them.

When Dickens was in Paris he found that
the *feuilleton* of the *Moniteur* contained daily

a French version of *Chuzzlewit*, and he wrote
to Forster on the 6th of January, 1856, "I
have already told you that I have received
a proposal from a responsible bookselling
house here [Paris] for a complete edition,
authorized by myself, of a French translation of all my books;" and on the 17th of
April he wrote to the same correspondent,
"On Monday I am going to dine with all
my translators at Hachette's, the bookseller who has made the bargain for the entire
edition."

Champs Elysées,
Tuesday, Twenty-second April, 1856.

MY DEAR COLLINS,—I have been quite
taken aback by your account of your alarm-
ing seizure; and have only become reas-
sured again, firstly, by the good-fortune of
your having left here and got so near your
doctor; secondly, by your hopefulness of
now making head in the right direction.
On the 3d or 4th I purpose being in town,
and I need not say that I shall forthwith
come to look after my old Patient.

On Sunday, to my infinite amazement,
Townshend appeared. He has changed his
plans, and is staying in Paris a week, before

going to Town for a couple of months. He
dined here on Sunday, and placidly ate and
drank in the most vigorous manner, and mild-
ly laid out a terrific perspective of projects
for carrying me off to the Theatre every
night. But in the morning he found himself with dawnings of Bronchitis, and is now
luxuriously laid up in lavender at his Hotel—
confining himself entirely to precious stones,
chicken, and fragrant wines qualified with
iced waters.

Last Friday I took Mrs. Dickens, Geor-
gina, and Mary and Katey, to dine at the
Trois frères. We then, sir, went off to the
Français to see *Comme il vous plaira*—which
is a kind of Theatrical Representation that
I think might be got up, with great com-
pleteness, by the Patients in the asylum for
Idiots. Dreariness is no word for it, vacan-
cy is no word for it, gammon is no word for
it, there *is* no word for it. Nobody has anything to do but to sit upon as many gray
stones as he can. When Jacques had sat
upon seventy - seven stones and forty - two
roots of trees (which was at the end of the
second act), we came away. He had by that

time been made violent love to by Celia, had shewn himself in every phase of his existence to be utterly unknown to Shakespeare, had made the speech about the Seven Ages out of its right place, and apropos of nothing on earth, and had in all respects conducted himself like a brutalized, benighted, and besotted Beast.

A wonderful dinner at Girardin's last Monday, with only one new (but appropriate) feature in it. When we went into the drawing-room after the banquet, which had terminated in a flower-pot out of a ballet being set before every guest, piled to the brim with the ruddiest fresh strawberries, he asked me if I would come into another room (a chamber of no account—rather like the last Scene in *Gustavus*) and smoke a cigar. On my replying yes, he opened, with a key attached to his watch-chain, a species of mahogany cave, which appeared to me to extend under the Champs Elysées, and in which were piled about four hundred thousand inestimable and unattainable cigars, in bundles or bales of about a thousand each.

Yesterday I dined at the bookseller's with

4

the body of Translators engaged on my new
Edition — one of them a lady, young and
pretty. (I hope, by-the-bye, judging from the
questions which they asked me and which I
asked them, that it will be really well done.)
Among them was an extremely amiable old
Savant, who occasionally expressed himself
in a foreign tongue which I supposed to be
Russian (I thought he had something to do
with the congress perhaps), but which my
host told me, when I came away, was English! We wallowed in an odd sort of dinner
which would have been splashy if it hadn't
been too sticky. Salmon appeared late in
the evening, and unforeseen creatures of the
lobster species strayed in after the pudding.
It was very hospitable and good-natured
though, and we all got on in the friendliest
way. Please to imagine me for three mor-
tal hours incessantly holding forth to the
translators, and, among other things, addressing them in a neat and appropriate
(French) speech. I came home quite light-
headed.

On Saturday night I paid three francs at
the door of that place where we saw the

wrestling, and went in, at 11 o'clock, to a
Ball. Much the same as our own National
Argyle Rooms. Some pretty faces, but all
of two classes—wicked and coldly calculat-
ing, or haggard and wretched in their worn
beauty. Among the latter was a woman of
thirty or so, in an Indian shawl, who never
stirred from a seat in a corner all the time I
was there. Handsome, regardless, brooding,
and yet with some nobler qualities in her
forehead. I mean to walk about to-night
and look for her. I didn't speak to her
there, but I have a fancy that I should like
to know more about her. Never shall, I
suppose.

Franconi's I have been to again, of course.
Nowhere else. I finished "that" No. as soon
as Macready went away, and have done
something for *Household Words* next week,
called *Proposals for a National Jest Book*,
that I take rather kindly to. The first
blank page of *Little Dorrit*, No. 8, now eyes
me on this desk with a pressing curiosity.
It will get nothing out of me to-day, I distinctly perceive.

That swearing of the Academy Carpenters

is the best thing of its kind I ever heard of.
I suppose the oath to be administered by
little Knight. It's my belief that the stout
Porter, now no more, wouldn't have taken it.
Our cook's going. Says she "ain't strong
enough for BooLone." I don't know what
there is particularly trying in that climate.
The nice little Nurse, who goes into all
manner of shops without knowing one word
of French, took some lace to be mended the
other day, and the Shopkeeper, impressed
with the idea that she had come to sell it,
would give her money; with which she re-
turned weeping, believing it (until explanation ensued) to be the price of shame.

All send kindest regard.

Ever faithfully,   C. D.

Ship Hotel, Dover,
Thirtieth April, 1856.

MY DEAR COLLINS,—Wills brought me
your letter this morning, and I am very
much interested in knowing what o'clock it
is by the Watch with the brass tail to it.
You know I am not in the habit of making
professions, but I have so strong an interest

in you and so true a regard for you that nothing can come amiss in the way of information as to your well-doing.

How I wish you were well now! For here I am in two of the most charming rooms (a third, a bedroom you could have occupied, close by), overlooking the sea in the gayest way. And here I shall be, for a change, till Saturday. And here we might have been, drinking confusion to Baronetcies, and re-solving never to pluck a leaf from the ·Toady Tree, till this very small world shall have rolled us off! Never mind. All to come — in the fulness of the Arctic Seasons.

I take, as the people say in the comedies of eighty years ago, "hugely" to the idea you have suggested to Wills. But you mustn't do anything until you feel it a pleasure; from which sensation (and the disap-pearance of the East Wind until next win-ter) I shall date your coming round the corner with a great velocity.

On Saturday morning I shall be in town about 11, and will come on to Howland Street about 1. Many thanks for your bulletin academical, which I have despatched straightway to Ary Scheffer.

They were all blooming in Paris yesterday morning. I took the Plorn out in a cabriolet the day before, and his observations on life in general were wonderful.

Ever yours,   · C. D.

On the 13th of July Dickens wrote to Collins from Boulogne as follows, concerning *The Diary of Anne Rodway*, by the latter, published in *Household Words* during that month: " I cannot tell you what a high opinion I have of *Anne Rodway*. . . . I read the first part at the office with strong admiration, and read the second on the railway coming back here. . . . My behavior before my fellow-passengers was weak in the extreme, for I cried as much as you could possibly desire. . . . I think it excellent, feel a personal pride and pleasure in it, which is a delightful sensation, and I know no one else who could have done it."

Boulogne,
Tuesday, Twenty-ninth July, 1856.

MY DEAR COLLINS,—I write you at once, in answer to yours received this morning, because there is a slight change in my London plans, necessitated by Townshend's intention of coming to the Pavilion here on the 5th or 6th, and hoping to have me pretty much at his disposal for a week or so.

Therefore, if Wills should purpose returning to London on Friday or on Saturday, I shall come up with him, and return here on the 4th or 5th of August. Will you hold yourself disengaged for next Sunday until you hear from me? I think I am very likely to be on the loose that day.

(Having done this morning, I am only waiting here for Wills, whom I don't like to despoil of his trip by going across now.)

On the 15th we shall, of course, delightedly expect you, and you will find your room in apple-pie order. I am charmed to hear you have discovered so good a notion for the play [*The Frozen Deep*]. Immense excitement is always in action here on the subject, and I don't think Mary and Katey will feel quite safe until you are shut up in the Pavilion on pen and ink.

I like that view of the picture controversy (what a World it is!) very much, and shall

be glad and much assisted if you will tell
me, *by return*, when you can have the copy
ready, and about how long it will be.   My
reason is this : to facilitate poor Wills's getting a holiday. . . .

We are getting more than usual in advance;
and if you can satisfy me on these points
while I have Wills beside me, I can keep a
No. open, and lead it off with that paper.

The château continues to be the best
known, and the Cook is really special.

All send their kindest regard, and their
welcome for the 15th on beforehand.

Ever faithfully,   C. D.

The Frozen Deep was produced on the an-
niversary of the birth of the younger Charles
Dickens, Twelfth night, 1857.   Dickens, writing concerning it on the 17th of January,
said : "We have just been acting a new play
of great merit, done in what I may call (mod-
estly speaking of the getting up and not of
the acting) an unprecedented way.   I believe that anything so complete has never
been seen.   We had an act at the North Pole,
where the slightest and greatest things the
eye beheld were equally taken from the

books of the polar voyagers. . . . It has been the talk of all London for these three weeks."

Mrs. W. H. Wills was a member of the dramatic company, and Mr. J. W. Francesco Berger undertook the musical part of the plays. Richard Wardour was the character assumed by Dickens.

Tavistock House.
Twelfth September, 1856.

MY DEAR COLLINS,—*An admirable idea.* It seems to me to supply and include everything the play wanted. But it is so very strong that I doubt whether the man can (without an anti-climax) be shewn to be rescued and alive until the last act. The struggle, the following him away, the great suspicion, and the suspended interest, in the second. The relief and joy of the discovery in the third.

Here, again, Mark's part seems to me to be suggested. An honest, bluff man, previously admiring and liking me—conceiving the terrible suspicion—watching its growth in his own mind—and gradually falling from me in the very generosity and manhood of his nature — would be engaging in itself, would be what he would do remarkably well; would give me capital things to do with him (and you know we go very well together), and would greatly strengthen the suspended interest aforesaid.

I throw this out with all deference, of course, to your internal view and preconception of the matter. Turn it how you will, the strength of the situation is *prodigious;* and if we don't bring the house down with it, I'm a—Tory (an illegible word which I mean for T-O-R-Y).

Hoping to see you to-night,

Ever cordially,   C. D.

Tavistock House, Saturday Night,
Thirteenth September, 1856.

MY DEAR COLLINS,—Another idea I have been waiting to impart. I dare say you have anticipated it. *Now*, Mrs. Wills's second sight is clear as to the illustration of it, and greatly helps that suspended interest. Thus: "You ask *me* what I see of those lost Voyagers. I see the lamb in the grasp of the lion —your bonnie bird alone with the hawk.

What do I see? I see you and all around you crying, Blood! The stain of his blood is upon you!" (C. D.)

Which would be right to a certain extent, and absolutely wrong as to the marrow of it.

Ever yours,   C. D.

Tavistock House,
Thursday, Ninth October, 1856.

MY DEAR COLLINS,—I should like to shew you some cuts I have made in the second act (subject to authorial sanction, of course). They are mostly verbal, and all bring the Play closer together.

Also, I should like to know whether it is likely that you will want to alter anything in these first two acts. If not, here are Charley, Mark, and I, all ready to write, and we may get a fair copy out of hand. From said fair copy all my people will write out their own parts.

I dine at home to-day, but not to-morrow. On Saturday, and Sunday likewise, I dine at home. We must perpetually " put ourselves in communication with the view of dealing with it "—as Wills says—the moment you

have done. How do you get on? And will
you come at 6 to-day—or when?

I am more sure than ever of the effect.

Ever faithfully,   C. D.

Tavistock House,
Fifteenth October, 1856.

MY DEAR COLLINS,—Will you read *Turning the Tables* (in my old Prompt-book) enclosed, and let me know whether you dare
to play Edgar de Courcy? There is very
good business in it with Humphreys (Mark).
My great difficulty is Patty Larkins.

Send me back the book when you answer.

Ever faithfully,   C. D.

.   .   .   .   .

P.P.S.—Here is *Animal Magnetism* to
read, too. Will you get another copy for
yourself at some theatrical shop? We play
it in two acts.

Tavistock House,
Sunday Night, Twenty-sixth October, 1856.

MY DEAR COLLINS,—Will you tell Pigott
of the Rehearsal arrangements when that
Ancient Mariner turns up?

Will you dine at our *H. W.* [*Household*

Words] Audit dinner, on Tuesday, the 4th of November, at ¼ past 5 ?

Will you come and see the ladies, in the rough, next Thursday at ½ past 7 ?

Though mayhap you may come here before, for you will be glad to know that Stanfield arrived from Holyhead at Midnight last night, and sent a Dispatch down here the first thing this morning, proposing to fall to, to-morrow. I have appointed him to be here at from 3 to ½ past to-morrow (Monday) afternoon to hear the Play; to dine at ½ past 5, and to go into the Theatre after dinner and settle his whole plans for the Carpenters. If you can come at the first of these times, or the second, or the third, it will be well. I have had an interview with the Authors, and printed them. I begin with the *Merry Berger* to-morrow night. I have found a very good farce (with character parts for all) in lieu of *Turning the Tables*. On the whole, have not been idle.

Ever faithfully,   C. D.

Took twenty miles to-day, and got up all Richard's words [Richard Wardour], to the

great terror of Finchley, Neasdon, Willesden,
and the adjacent country.

Tavistock House,
Saturday Evening, First November, 1856.

MY DEAR COLLINS,—Forster came here
yesterday afternoon to ask me if he might
read the Play, and I lent it to him.   This
afternoon I got the enclosed from him (which
please to read at this point).   You know·
that I don't agree with him as to the Nurse.
... But I think his suggestion that the going
away of the women might be suggested at
the close of the First act as a preparation
for the last an excellent one.   Will you think
of it?   By an alteration that we could make
in a quarter of an hour it might be done ;
and, moreover—this suggestion upon a suggestion arises in my mind—it might be made
the Nurse's position in the Play that her
blood-red Second Sight *is the first occasion of
their going away at all.*   (Forster does not
clearly understand the circumstances of their
going ; but never mind that).

His notion that Clara tells too much has
been strong in my mind since I first got that

act in Rehearsal. But, doubtful whether it might not unconsciously arise in me from a paternal interest in my own part, I had, as yet, said nothing about it—the rather as I had not yet seen the Second act on the stage.

Stanfield wants to cancel the chair altogether, and to substitute a piece of rock on the ground, composing with the Cavern. That, I take it, is clearly an improvement. He has a happy idea of painting the ship which is to take them back, ready for sailing, on the sea.

Nothing could induce [William] Telbin yesterday to explain what he was going to do before Stanfield ; and nothing would induce Stanfield to explain what *he* was going to do before Telbin. But they had every inch and curve and line in that bow accurately measured by the carpenters, and each requested to have a drawing of the whole made to scale. Then each said that he would make his model in card-board, and see what I "thought of it." I have no doubt the thing will be as well done as it can be.

Will you dine with us at 5 on Monday before Rehearsal?   We can then talk over
Forster's points.   If you are disengaged on
Wednesday, shall we breathe some fresh air
in dilution of Tuesday's "alcohol," and walk
through the fallen leaves in Cobham Park?
I can then explain how I think you can get
your division of the Christmas No. [*Wreck
of the Golden Mary*] very originally and nat-
urally.   It came into my head to-day.

Ever faithfully,   C. D.

P.S.—I re-open this to say that I find from
Wills that next Tuesday being the Audit Day
at all is his mistake.   It is Tuesday *week*.
Therefore, if Tuesday is a fine day, shall we
go out then?

Tavistock House,
Friday, Fourteenth November, 1856.

MY DEAR COLLINS,—I could not send you
the books before I went out this morning
for a 12-miler, the collection being curiously
spare in pick-up cases, and it being a work
of time to find them.

Will you exchange proofs of the *Captain*
[first part of *The Wreck of the Golden Mary*]
with me?   The proofs you have have mark-

ings of mine upon them which will be useful to me in correcting. You can bring me those when you come to-night.

Ever faithfully,   C. D.

Tavistock House,
Tuesday Evening, Sixteenth December, 1856.

MY DEAR COLLINS,—I send round to ascertain that you are all right. Not that I have any misgiving on the subject, for when I shook hands with you last night you were as cool and comfortable as an unlucky Dog could be.

All progressing satisfactorily. Telbin painting on the Stage. Carpenters knocking down the Drawing-room.

We are obliged to do *Animal Magnetism* on Thursday evening at 8. If you are strong enough to come, I know you will; if you are not, I know you won't.

Ever cordially,   C. D.

Tavistock House,
Saturday, Tenth January, 1857.

MY DEAR COLLINS,—On second thoughts I am afraid of wasting the spirits of the company by calling the Dance at 6 on Monday.

5

Therefore I abandon that intention.   I hope we may get it right by speaking to one another in the Dressing-room.

On Play Days (only two more—how they fly !) Mark and I dine at 3, off steak and stout, at the Cock, in Fleet Street.   If you should be disposed to join us, then and there you'll find us.   Ever cordially,   C. D.

The MS. of *The Frozen Deep* was sold at auction in London in the summer of 1890 for three hundred guineas.   Collins had added four pages of Introduction and a copy of the printed bill of the performance which was given in Manchester in August, 1857, for the benefit of the family of Douglas Jerrold, who had lately passed away.   In the Manchester cast were Egg, Lemon, Shirley Brooks, Charles and Wilkie Collins, and Charles Dickens.   In this Introduction Collins said : " Mr. Dickens himself played the principal part, and played it with a truth, vigor, and pathos never to be forgotten by those who were fortunate enough to witness it. . . . At Manchester this play was twice performed ; on the second evening before three thousand people.   This was, I think, the finest of all its representations.   The extraordinary intelligence and enthusiasm of the great audience stimulated us all to do our best. Dickens surpassed himself. He literally electrified the audience." Collins rewrote the play, and read it in Boston in the spring of 1874 as "a Special Farewell" to America, prefacing it with a short speech, in which he said that he understood it had already been produced at a Boston theatre (although then never printed) without his knowledge, and, of course, without his consent.

Dickens took possession of Gad's Hill Place in the month of June, 1857. In September he visited the north of England with Collins, where Collins sprained one of his ankles severely, and where and when they concocted and began *The Lazy Tour of Two Idle Apprentices*—contributed jointly to *Household Words* in October. After their return they wrote, together, for the Christmas number of the same periodical, *The Perils of Certain English Prisoners, and Their Treasure in Women, Children, Silver, and Jewels*, the manuscript of which was sold in 1890 for two hundred pounds. It is one of the few pieces of the Dickens MSS. not bequeathed by Forster to the English nation. Of this Dickens wrote Chapters I. and III.;

Collins, Chapter II., a fragment of which is here reproduced in fac-simile, while the copy of each is crowded with many notes and corrections by both hands. The original sketch for the story was written by Collins, and contains hints and suggestions by the head of the literary copartnership, who also wrote the title-page, to which Collins added a few explanatory notes. On the 6th of February, 1858, Dickens sent the following note :

My dear Wilkie,—Thinking it may one day be interesting to you—say when you are weak in *both* feet, and when I and Doncaster are quiet, and the great race is over —to possess this little memorial of our joint Christmas work, I have put it together for you, and now send it on its coming home from the Binder.   Faithfully yours,

CHARLES DICKENS.

Tavistock House,
Monday, Nineteenth January, 1857.

My dear Collins,—Will you come and dine here next Sunday at 5 ?

There is no one coming but a poor little Scotchman, domiciled in America—a musical composer and singer—who .brought me

7

83

II. The Prisoner & the Woods.

There we all slept, huddled up on the bench under the burning sun, with the priest closing us in on every side—no prison a company of highly...maginative men, women, and children, as we were gathered together and... my nation is the world. Of the mass of comfort there were thirteen in all; many matters on for my being loved as well as dreaming of the woman time was of them. Of the children, including his honor of those, there were... detectives, thirty-five living male, ... and ... on the very back of another... I kept my temper & ... myself entirely, but when we ... were...ed on the back of the... the moment I have devised, I did not... in my heart believe that anyone of our lives was worth four minutes' purchase.

a letter yesterday from New York, and quite moved me by his simple tale of loneliness. He is——, softened by trouble, with all the starch out of his collar, and all the money out of his Bank.

O reaction, reaction !

Ever faithfully,   C. D.

Tavistock House,
Fourteenth February, 1857.

MY DEAR COLLINS,—Will you come and dine at the office on Thursday at ¼ past 5 ? We will then discuss the Brighton or other trip possibilities. I am tugging at my Oar too—should like a change—find the Galley a little heavy—must stick to it—am generally in a collinsion state.

Ever faithfully,   C. D.

Tavistock House,
Wednesday, Fourth March, 1857.

MY DEAR COLLINS,—*I cannot tell you* what pleasure I had in the receipt of your letter yesterday evening, or how much good it did me in the depression consequent upon an exciting and exhausting day's work. I im-

mediately arose (like the desponding Princes
in the *Arabian Nights*, when the old woman — Procuress evidently, and probably of
French extraction—comes to whisper about
the Princesses they love) and washed my
face and went out; and my face has been
shining ever since.

Ellis [proprietor of the Bedford Hotel at
Brighton] responds to my letter that rooms
shall be ready! There is a train at 12
which appears to me to be the train for
the distinguished visitors. If you will call
for me in a cab at about 20 minutes past
11, my hand will be on the latch of the
door.

I have got a book to take down with me
of which I have not read a line, but which I
have been saving up to get a pull at it in the
nature of a draught—*The Dead Secret*—by
a Fellow Student.

Plornish has broken ground with a Joke
which I consider equal to Sydney Smith.

Ever faithfully,
CHARLES DICKENS.

Tavistock House,
Monday Evening, Eleventh May, 1857.

MY DEAR COLLINS,—I am very sorry that we shall not have you to-morrow. Think you would get on better if you were to come, after all.

Yes, sir; thank God, I *have* finished! [*Little Dorrit*]. On Sunday last I wrote the two little words of three letters each.

Any mad proposal you please will find a wildly insane response in

Yours ever,   C. D.

We shall have to arrange about Tuesday at Gad's Hill. You remember the engagement?

Tavistock House,
Friday Evening, Twenty-second May, 1857.

MY DEAR COLLINS,—Hooray!!!

From our lofty heights let us look down on the toiling masses with mild complacency—with gentle pity—with dove-eyed benignity.

To-morrow I am bound to Forster; on Sunday to solemn Chief Justice's, in remote fastnesses beyond Norwood; on Monday to

Geographical Societies dining to cheer on Lady Franklin's Expedition; on Tuesday to Procter's; on Wednesday, sir—on Wednesday—if the mind can devise anything sufficiently in the style of sybarite Rome in the days of its culminating voluptuousness, I am your man.

Shall we appoint to meet at the *House-hold Words* office at ¼ past 5? I have an appointment with Russel [W. H.] at 3 that afternoon, which *may*, but which I don't think will, detain me a few minutes after my time. In that unlikely case, will you wait for me at the office?

If you can think of any tremendous way of passing the night, in the mean time, do. I don't care what it is. I give (for that night only) restraint to the Winds!

I am very much excited by what you tell me of Mr. F.'s aunt.* I already look upon her as mine. Will you bring her with you?

Wills tells me that he thinks the princi-

[* A picture by an artist named Gale, of that character in *Little Dorrit*, and bought by Charles Dickens through Collins.]

ples of story-writing are scarcely understood
in this age and Empire.

Ever faithfully,   C. D.

No. 16, Wellington Street, North, Strand,
First June (Monday), 1857.

MY DEAR COLLINS,—In consequence of
bedevilments at Gad's Hill, arising from the
luggage wandering over the face of the earth,
I shall have to pass to-morrow behind a
hedge, attired in leaves from my own fig-tree.
Will you therefore consider our appointment
to stand for next day—Wednesday?

When last heard of the family itself (including the birds and the goldfinch on his
perch) had been swept away from the stu-
pefied John by a crowd of Whitsun holi-
day-makers, and had gone (without tickets)
somewhere down into Sussex. A desperate
calmness has fallen upon me. I don't care.

Faithfully ever,   C. D.

H. W. Office,
Sixteenth June, 1857.

MY DEAR COLLINS,—What an unlucky
fellow you are! What a foot you have for
putting into anything!

I write this to Harley Place, having been
unable to write yesterday.   I must be in
town on Thursday, and will come up to you.
I will try to come at about 12.

Mrs. Wills's lameness makes a new Esther
the first thing wanted.   You once said you
knew a lady who could and would have done
it.   Is that lady producible?

Ever faithfully,   C. D.

Tavistock House,
Friday Night, Twenty-sixth June, 1857.

MY DEAR COLLINS,—I am so sensible of
that First Act's requiring—for the old hands
—so much care in a less feverish atmos-
phere than the Theatre, that I must propose Rehearsals of the Ladies here (our
house is stripped, and has plenty of room),
on Tuesday, Wednesday, and Thursday. The
hour must rest principally with Mrs. Dickinson, but I should like it best in the evening—say at 8.   However, my time is the
Play's.   There is a great deal at stake, and
it *must be* well done. Will you see Mrs. Dickinson between this and Monday's rehearsal,
and consult her convenience on the point?

I shall be at the Gallery during the greater part of to-morrow, and shall dine at the Garrick at 6, before going to the Concert.

Ever faithfully, C. D.

Tavistock House,
Sunday Morning, Second August, 1857.

MY DEAR COLLINS,—I write this on my way back to Gad's Hill from Manchester.

As our sum is not made up, and as I had urgent Deputation and so forth from Manchester Magnates at the reading on Friday night, I have arranged to act the *Frozen Deep* in the Free Trade Hall, on Friday and Saturday nights, the 21st and 22d. It is *animmense place*, and we shall be obliged to have actresses — though I have written to our friend, Mrs. Dickinson, to say that I don't fear her, if she likes to play with them. (I am already trying to get the best who *have been* on the stage.)

Whether Charley can play his part or not, I will tell him to let you know directly.

I had a letter from the Olympic the other day, begging me to go to a rehearsal. I have appointed next Friday, if agreeable and convenient.   In haste,

Ever faithfully,   C. D.

Garrick Club,
Monday Evening, Seventeenth August, 1857.

MY DEAR COLLINS,—Fred Evans's grand-mother being evidently on the point of Death, no Evans is available (as I learn on coming to town to-night) for Manchester. This leaves to be supplied Easel and Bateson. I immediately think of your brother Charles and Luard. If it had been a purely managerial and not personal case, I should have proposed to Luard to do one of the parts and to your brother to do the other. But I think it right that Charles Collins should first select for himself. Now, will you, before you come to the Rehearsal to-morrow, arrange with him whether he will play one—which one—or both ; and if he leaves one, will you call on Luard as you come down and offer that one to him ?

I write at Express pace, but you will understand all I mean.

Ever faithfully,   C. D.

Tavistock House,
Saturday, Twenty-ninth August, 1857.

MY DEAR COLLINS,—Partly in the grim despair and restlessness of this subsidence from excitement, and partly for the sake of *Household Words*, I want to cast about whether you and I can go anywhere—take any tour—see anything—whereon we could write something together. Have you any idea tending to any place in the world? Will you rattle your head and see if there is any pebble in it which we could wander away and play at marbles with? We want something for *Household Words*, and I want to escape from myself. For, when I *do* start up and stare myself seedily in the face, as happens to be my case at present, my blankness is inconceivable — indescribable — my misery amazing.

I shall be in town on Monday. Shall we talk then? Shall we talk at Gad's Hill? *What* shall we do? As I close this I am on my way back by train.

Ever faithfully,   C. D.

Dickens devoted himself for many months

during the year 1858 to public readings in the provinces of Great Britain.

Tavistock House,
Tavistock Square, London, W. C.,
Tuesday night, Twenty-fifth May, 1858.

MY DEAR WILKIE,—A thousand thanks for your kind letter. I always feel your friendship very much, and prize it in proportion to the true affection I have for you.

Your letter comes to me only to-night. Can you come round to me in the morning (Wednesday) before 12 ? I can then tell you all in lieu of writing. It is rather a long story—over, I hope, now.

Ever affectionately,   C. D.

Gad's Hill Place,
Higham by Rochester, Kent,
Sunday, First August, 1858.

MY DEAR WILKIE,—I am off from here to-day, and enclose you (hastily) my Tour, and my address at each place. I hope you are enjoying yourself at Broadstairs—holding on by your great advance in health—and getting into the condition, physically, of Ben Caunt—morally, of William Shakespeare.

Wilkie Collins

Charley's [Charles Collins] paper has a great deal in it that is very droll and good. I have sent it to the Printer.

With kind regards, ever affec'ly,

CHARLES DICKENS.

Swan Hotel, Worcester,
Wednesday Evening, Eleventh August, 1858.

MY DEAR WILKIE,—I have just now toned down the capital unknown Public article a little, here and there. Not because I dispute its positions, but because there are some things (true enough) that it would not be generous in me, as a novelist and a periodical editor, to put too prominently forward. You will not find it essentially changed anywhere.

Your letter gave me great pleasure, as all letters that you write me are sure to do. But the mysterious addresses, O misconstructive one, merely refer to places where Arthur Smith did not know aforehand the names of the best Hotels. . . .

We have done exceedingly well since we have been out—with this remarkable (and pleasant) incident, that wherever I read

6

twice, the turn-away is invariably on the second occasion. They don't quite understand beforehand what it is, I think, and expect a man to be sitting down in some corner, droning away like a mild bagpipe. In that large room at Clifton, for instance, the people were perfectly taken off their legs by *The Chimes*—started—looked at each other—started again—looked at me—and then burst into a storm of applause. I think the best audiences I have yet had were at Exeter and Plymouth—at Exeter, the best I have ever seen; at Plymouth I read three times, twice in one day. A better morning audience for little Dombey could not be. And the Boots at night was a shout all through.

I cannot deny that I shall be heartily glad when it is all over, and that I miss the thoughtfulness of my quiet room and desk. But perhaps it is best for me not to have it just now, and to wear and toss my storm away—or as much of it as will ever calm down while the water rolls—in this restless manner.

Arthur Smith knows I am writing to you, and sends his kindest regard. He is all usefulness and service. I never could have done without him—should have left the un-redeemed Bills on the walls and taken flight.

This is a stupid letter, but I write it before dressing to read, and you know what a brute I am at such times.

Ever affectionately, C. D.

P.S.—I miss Richard Wardour's dress, and always want to put it on. I would rather, by a great deal, act. Apropos of which, I think I have a very fine notion of a part. It shall be yours.

On the 6th of September he wrote to Collins from Gad's Hill:

" Do you see your way to making a Christmas number of this idea that I am going very briefly to hint? Some disappointed person, man or woman, prematurely disgusted with the world, for some reason or no reason (the person should be young, I think) retires to an old lonely house, or an old lonely mill, or anything you like, with one attendant, resolved to shut out the world and hold

no communion with it. The one attendant
sees the absurdity of the idea, pretends to
humor it, but really thus to slaughter it.
Everything that happens, everybody that
comes near, every breath of human interest
that floats into the old place from the vil-
lage, or the heath, or the four cross-roads
near which it stands, and from which be-
lated travellers stray into it, shows beyond
mistake that you can't shut out the world;
that you are in it, to be of it; that you get
into a false position the moment you try to
sever yourself from it; and that you must
mingle with it and make the best of it, and
make the best of yourself in the bargain. If
we could plot out a way of doing this together, I would not be afraid to take my
part. If we could not, could we plot out a
way of doing it, and taking in other stories
by other hands? If we could not do either
(but I think we could), shall we fall back
upon a round of stories again?"

The result was *A House to Let*, to which
Dickens contributed the chapter "Going
into Society."

Royal Hotel, Southampton,
Tuesday Evening, Ninth November, 1858.

MY DEAR WILKIE,—I was under the impression that I was to finish at Brighton on the *afternoon* of Saturday. I find, however, that I read both in the afternoon and in the evening. I would propose to you to come and celebrate the end of the Tour by dining with us that day at the Bedford; but, between two readings, I am afraid it would rather bore than gratify your digestive functions.

Assuming it not to be worth your while to take a Saturday "Return" to Brighton, then will you arrange to go down to Gad's Hill on Sunday in good time for dinner? I will go down by some train or other in good time for dinner, too. How do you feel about having the big bedroom, and writing there through the week? I would go to work too, and we might do Heaven knows how much, with an escapade to town for a night, if we felt in the humour.

I pause for a reply. Let me find it at the Bedford at Brighton, when I get there on Friday forenoon.

Wills arranged with me that you were presently to receive sacks of Christmas "matter"—not much "mind" with it, I am afraid. . . .

Ever affectionately,
CHARLES DICKENS.

WILKIE COLLINS, Esquire.

Bedford Hotel,
Saturday, Thirteenth November, 1858.

MY DEAR WILKIE,—I am reading this afternoon. Dinner is ordered at 5 punctually. They will shew you up into the sitting-room when you have read this, and will also shew you your bedroom, which I have duly commanded. Think of our finding ready-taken here *one thousand Stalls!*

Ever affectionately,　C. D.

In the year 1859 Dickens incorporated *Household Words* with *All the Year Round,* giving the new and joint periodical the latter title. The initial number appeared on the 30th of April, and contained the first chapter of *The Tale of Two Cities.* To *All the Year Round* Collins contributed *The Queen of Hearts,* a collection of short stories published in 1859, and *The Woman in White*, published the next year. Concerning the latter novel, Dickens wrote to Collins January 7, 1859, as follows :

"I have read this book with great care and attention. There can be no doubt that it is a very great advance on all your former writing, and most especially in respect of tenderness. In character it is excellent. Mr. Fairlie is as good as the lawyer, and the lawyer as good as he. Mr. Vesey and Miss Holcombe, in their different ways, equally meritorious. Sir Percival also is most skilfully shown, though I doubt (you see what small points I come to) whether any man ever showed uneasiness by hand or foot without being forced by nature to show it in his face too. The story is very interesting, and the writing of it admirable."

Tavistock House,
Tavistock Square, London, W. C.
Wednesday, Twenty-sixth January, 1859.

MY DEAR WILKIE,—Look over the jotted titles on the other side, that we may discuss them to-morrow. It is the very first thing to settle.   I can make no way until I have got a name.   Ever affec'ly,   C. D.

> Query.—ONCE A WEEK.
>   ALL THE YEAR ROUND.
>   1.   Weekly Bells.
>   2.   The Forge.
>   3.   Evergreen Leaves.

If "The Forge" only, some *motto*, explaining title—something like "We beat out our ideas on this."

ONCE A WEEK.

The Hearth.
The Forge . . . . this.
The Crucible.
The Anvil of the Time.
Charles Dickens's Own (like an Entertainment).
Seasonable Leaves.
Evergreen Leaves . . . . . . this.
Home.
Home Music.
Change.
Time and Tide.
Twopence.

English Bells.
Weekly Bells . . . . this
The Rocket!
Good Humour.

No. 11, Wellington St., North, Strand,
London, W. C.,
Saturday, Ninth April, 1859.

MY DEAR WILKIE,—The insertions in the
enclosed just supply what was wanting. But
will you make one more alteration in it, or
the title will not by any means fit in among
the other titles—such an alteration as will
admit of the paper's being called:

Sure to be Healthy, Wealthy, and Wise.

We want the Proof as soon as possible.

You will receive to - night the *Occasional
Register,* for which I have dotted down a
few paragraphs. Pray say if you can do
anything for it. It is grievously wanted for
the 1st No. The said 1st No. *must* be made
up and sent to the Printer's in good time
on Monday. On Tuesday afternoon I shall
go over it finally. Will you come here then?
And will you let me know, at Tavistock

House, whether we shall dine somewhere afterwards?

Ever faithfully,   C. D.

Gad's Hill Place,
Higham by Rochester, Kent,
Sunday, Twelfth June, 1859.

MY DEAR WILKIE,—I really am exceedingly sorry to find that you have been so unwell again. Let us talk the Malvern matter well over here. My experience of that treatment induces me to hold that it is wonderfully efficacious *where there is great constitutional vitality;* where there is not, I think it may be a little questionable.

Whenever you decide to come your room will be ready for you, and you will give us (as you know you always do) great pleasure. Our Charley, I think, will come down on Wednesday—so shall I—at 20 minutes past 2.

Wills and I will dine with you (since you propose it) to-morrow. Shall we say *half past five* sharp?

The "cold" is pretty much in the old state, so I have made up my mind to think no more of it, and to go (in a general way) the way of all flesh.

Ever affec'ly,   C. D.

Gad's Hill Place,
Higham by Rochester, Kent,
Sunday, Seventeenth July, 1859.

MY DEAR WILKIE,—My plans are not defined, but I *think* I shall stay in London Tuesday night. That is no reason, however, for your fixing in the Metropolis of the world, the Emporium of commerce, and free home of the Slave. Therefore I shall leave word here that the Basket is to meet you at the Higham Station by the train *which leaves London at* 9 *on Tuesday evening.*

Ever affec'ly,   C. D.

Gad's Hill Place,
Higham by Rochester, Kent.
Thursday Night, Twenty-fifth August, 1859.

MY DEAR WILKIE,—This is written on a most intensely hot night, with rain and lightning, and with shoals of little tortoises (only harder in substance) dashing in at the window, and trying in vain to smash themselves on this paper—that was one. He is now beating his eyelids to powder (I am happy to say) on the obdurate black slab of the inkstand.

I am not quite well—can't get quite well; have an instinctive feeling that nothing but sea air and sea water will set me right. I want to come to Broadstairs next Wednesday by the mid-day train and stay till Monday. As I must work every morning, will you ask the Noble Ballard [landlord of the Albion Hotel, Broadstairs] (he will contradict you, but never mind that) if he can reserve a comfortable bedroom and quiet *writeable-in* sitting-room, for those days, for his ancient friend and patron. Then you two can dine with me one day—I can dine with you another — and evenings similarly arranged. Another tortoise, two earwigs, and a spider. Will you write to me here, after seeing the gallant host of the Albion? Dine with me on the first day, and tell him we dine, or it will break his heart.

What do you mean by not answering my beautiful letter from the office?

Love from all. Ever affectionately,

C. D.

Gad's Hill Place,
Higham by Rochester, Kent,
Thursday, Sixth October, 1859.

MY DEAR WILKIE,—I do not positively say
that the point you put might not have been
done in your manner; but I have a very strong
conviction that it would have been overdone
in that manner — too elaborately trapped,
baited, and prepared — in the main anticipated, and its interest wasted.   This is
quite apart from the peculiarity of the Doctor's [Dr. Manette—*A Tale of Two Cities*]
character, as affected by his imprisonment;
which of itself would, to my thinking, render it quite out of the question to put the
reader inside of him before the proper time,
in respect of matters that were dim to himself through being in a diseased way, mor-
bidly shunned by him.   I think the business of art is to lay all that ground carefully,
not with the care that conceals itself—to
shew, by a backward light, what everything
has been working to—but only to *suggest*,
until the fulfilment comes.   These are the
ways of Providence, of which ways all art is
but a little imitation.

"Could it have been done at all, in the way I suggest, to advantage?" is your question. I don't see the way, and I never have seen the way, is my answer. I cannot imagine it that way, without imagining the reader wearied and the expectation Wire-drawn.

I am very glad you liked it so much. It has greatly moved and excited me in the doing, and Heaven knows I have done my best and believed in it.

Ever affect'ly yours,   C. D.

Gad's Hill Place,
Higham by Rochester, Kent,
Sunday, Twenty-ninth July, 1860.

MY DEAR WILKIE,—Let me send you my heartiest congratulations on your having come to the end of your (as yet) last labor, and having triumphantly finished your best book [*The Woman in White*]. I presume that the undersigned obedient disciple may read it *now?*

Let us dine at the office on Tuesday at 5. I am free until half past 7.

I am something worn to-day by a sad expedition to Manchester and back. Perhaps

Wills has told you that poor Alfred [Dickens] is dead.

Ever affectionately,   C. D.

Dickens finished *Great Expectations* in 1861, and contributed three of the seven chapters of *Tom Tiddler's Ground* to the Christmas number of *All the Year Round*, which began that year the serial publication of Bulwer's *Strange Story*. In October he lost by death his friend Arthur Smith—his manager and companion during his provincial wanderings—of whom he wrote to Forster in 1857: "I have got hold of Arthur Smith as the best man of business I know." And in the autumn of 1861 he wrote to his daughter: "Poor dear Arthur is a sad loss to me, and indeed I was very fond of him. But the readings must be fought out, like all the rest of life."

A close examination of the news and advertising columns of the London daily and weekly journals has resulted in no hint as to the nature of the allusion to "last night" made by Dickens in the following letter. Collins evidently delivered his maiden speech at some function, but the dinner of The Literary Fund was eaten a few nights before, and a banquet at the Mansion House to the Guild of Literature and Art was not given until a night or two later. Collins no doubt was present on both occasions; but it is not recorded in the public prints that he spoke at either.

Lord Warden Hotel, Dover,
Friday Evening, Twenty-fourth May, 1861.

MY DEAR WILKIE,—I am delighted to receive so good an account of last night, and have no doubt that it was a thorough success. Now it is over, I may honestly say that I am glad you were (by your friendship) forced into the Innings, for there is no doubt that it is of immense importance to a public man in our way to have his wits at his tongue's end. Sir (as Dr. Johnson would have said), if it be not irrational in man to count his feathered bipeds before they are hatched, we will conjointly astonish them next year. *Boswell:* Sir, I hardly understand you. *Johnson:* Sir, you never understand anything. *Boswell* (in a sprightly manner): Perhaps, sir, I am all the better for it. *Johnson* (savagely): Sir, I do not know but that you are. There is Lord Carlisle (smiling); he never understands anything, and yet the dog's well enough. Then, sir, there is Forster; he understands many things, and yet the fellow is fretful. Again, sir, there is Dickens, with a facile way with him—like Davy, sir, like Davy—yet I am told that the man is lying at a hedge ale-house by the sea-shore in Kent, as long as they will trust him. *Boswell:* But there are no hedges by the sea in Kent, sir. *Johnson:* And why not, sir? *Boswell* (at a loss): I don't know, sir, unless— *Johnson* (thunder-ing): Let us have no unlesses, sir. If your father had never said "unless," he would never have begotten you, sir. *Boswell* (yield-ing): Sir, that is very true.

Of course I am dull and penitent here, but it is very beautiful. I can work well, and I walked, by the cliffs, to Folkestone and back to-day, when it was so exquisitely beautiful that, though I was alone, I could not keep silence on the subject. In the four-teen miles I doubt if I met twelve people. They say this house is full, yet I meet no-body, save now and then a languishing youth in a loose, very blue coat, lounging at the door and sucking the round head of a

7

cane, as if he were trying the fit before he had it cut off from the stem as a pill, and swallowed it.

I hope—begin to hope—that somewhere about the 12th of June will see me out of the book [*Great Expectations*]. I am anxious for some days at Gad's Hill, and settlement of Christmas No. with you. The idea I have will certainly do, I think, and save us a quantity of beating about.

At the end of this next week I will write again. I think we may book Wednesday Week, safely, for the office.

I can hardly see, it is getting so dark.

[Benjamin] Webster is a thorough good fellow. You know how often I have said so. There are better and finer qualities in him than in a host of men.

Gad's Hill Place,
Higham by Rochester, Kent,
Sunday, Twenty-third June, 1861.

MY DEAR WILKIE,—We will arrange our Xmas No., please God, under the shade of the Oak Trees.

I· shall remain in town on the Thursday, and will return with you on the Friday. We can settle our Train when we meet on Wednesday.

As yet, I have hardly got into the enjoyment of thorough laziness. Bulwer was so very anxious that I should alter the end of *Great Expectations* — the extreme end, I mean, after Biddy and Joe are done with— and stated his reasons so well, that I have resumed the wheel and taken another turn at it. Upon the whole, I think it is for the better. You shall see the change when we meet.

The country is most charming and this place very pretty. I am sorry to hear that the hot East winds have taken such a devastating blow into No. 12 Harley Street. They have been rather surprising, if anything in weather can be said to surprise.

I don't know whether anything remarkable comes off in the air to-day; but the blue-bottles (there are 9 in this room) are all banging their heads against the window-glass in the most astonishing manner. I think there must be some competitive examination somewhere, and these nine have been rejected. Ever affect'ly, C. D.

P. S.—I reopen this to state that the most madly despondent blue-bottle has committed suicide, and fallen dead on the carpet.

Gad's Hill Place,
Higham by Rochester, Kent,
Friday, Twelfth July, 1861.

MY DEAR WILKIE,—. . . It happens very unfortunately that I cannot get to Broadstairs before Thursday. As soon as the [John] Leeches go (they came yesterday, and will probably stay till Monday) I must look after some matters in town, where I think I shall remain all next week. When I hoped to come, I thought you were intending to remain longer. My hope shall now be transferred to the shore on which you *do* remain.

Lowestoft has improved very much since I was there, and no doubt has now a good hotel and good houses. But it did not impress me favorably, by reason of the Sea's coming in shallow, and going out over moist, sandy plain a long way. In this particular I seem to remember it as a more saline and removed Southend. . . .

Bulwer was great here, and perfectly enjoyed himself. You will be amazed when you see what he has done with his first four numbers—all I have read—and with what curious patience, study, and skill he has gone into the art of the Weekly No. There is a remarkably skilfully done woman, one of Mrs. Colonel Poyntz. The whole idea of the story turned in a masterly way towards the safe point of the compass.

I have been paying bills all the morning, and must send this dull reply to your amusing letter perforce, as I must now appear in the Leech hemisphere. No doubt I shall see or hear from you in town, and know your movements. I am so horribly lazy that I have done nothing and thought nothing since you went away. . . .

Wills told us a story here yesterday that I thought very ridiculous, about a charity-boy who persisted in saying to the Inspector of Schools that Our Saviour was the only forgotten son of his father, and that he was forgotten by his father before all worlds, &c., &c., in an Athanasian and Theological dogmatism.

Ever affectionately,   C. D.

The Great White Horse, Ipswich,
Thursday, Thirty-first October, 1861.

MY DEAR WILKIE,—On coming here just
now (half past one) I found your letter awaiting me, and it gave me infinite pleasure—
you can scarcely think how much pleasure ;
for to hold consultation on the quiet pur-
suits in which we have had so much common interest for a long time now is a delightful and wholesome thing in the midst
of this kind of life — in the midst of any
kind of life.

I entirely agree with you as to the neces-
sity of writing up the compact concerning
the people who come in at the gate [*Tom
Tiddler's Ground*]. I have not the least
doubt that it is hurried and huddled up as
I have written it, and that much more can
be made of it. Much more, therefore (please
God), *shall* be made of it when we get to
work.

The child notion enchants me. With my
love for the blessed children, I could sit
down and do it out of hand, if I could do
anything with the gas-lights of the night
looming in the 8 o'clock future. But when

I get to the sea next week I hope so to turn
the notion over as to be able to work upon
it when I come back briskly and quickly. I
have no doubt about it, accept it, and devote myself to it! (Here I raise my hand
to Heaven.)

I think *Our Hidden Selves* a very good
title—but I also think a better can come of
it. I am not sure. Now I quite discern
where your notion tends, I will try if I can
find a better.

The first night at Norwich was a dismal beginning—altogether unwonted and strange.
We had not a good Let, and (the place of
reading being a great, cold, stone-paved
Gothic Hall) the Audience appeared to be
afraid of me and of each other. I was out
of sorts. Everything seemed forlorn and
strange to me. Poor dear Arthur gone, and
the very wind in the arches (——them!)
seeming to howl about it. As a very little
thing would have stirred me, in such a state
of mind, to do my best, so a very little thing
stirred me to do my worst—and, on the
whole, I think I did it.

Next night was Nickleby and the Trial.

I had had a good walk in the bright air, and time to reason myself up a bit. There was a brilliant Audience, and I think I must report of Nickleby that, for a certain fantastic and hearty enjoyment, it tops all the Readings. The people were really quite ridiculous to see when Squeers read the boys' letters. And I am inclined to suspect that the impression of protection and hope derived from Nickleby's going away protecting Smike is exactly the impression — this is discovered by chance — that an Audience most likes to be left with.

Last night I read Copperfield at Bury St. Edmunds to a very fine Audience. I don't think a word—not to say an idea—was lost; and I am confirmed in my impression that it will be a very great card indeed in London.

From Brighton I will write you again, suggesting the course of proceeding for the Xmas No. in my ten or eleven days of reserve. Until then and ever, believe me,

Affectionately,

CHARLES DICKENS.

WILKIE COLLINS, Esquire.

Stick to cold water and the brush-gloves,

and my life upon it they will do good to those secretions!

Collins was engaged upon *No Name* in 1862 ; and the Christmas story was *Somebody's Luggage*, to which, by reason of a severe illness, he was able to contribute nothing.

Gad's Hill Place,
Higham by Rochester, Kent,
Sunday, January Fourth, 1862.

MY DEAR WILKIE,—When I proposed Thursday for the office I forgot that a choice between Thursday and Friday was given to the Forsters for our going there. I am reminded of it this morning by their writing to fix Thursday. Therefore, will you say *Friday* for the office, and at half past 5 instead of 6? . . .

It is pretty clear to me that you must go in for a regular pitched battle with that rheumatic gout. Don't be satisfied with Frank Beard's patching you, now that you have leisure, but be set up afresh. I don't like that notion of the eight and forty hours. It's not a long enough time, and the treatment *in* the time must be too ferocious.

Nature does not proceed in that way, and is not to be proceeded with in that way. With all respect for my Hon. friend M. R. C. S. [Member Royal College of Surgeons], I think it a demonstrable mistake, and I hope you will arrive at the same conclusion.

In the *A. Y. R.* [*All the Year Round*] matter I did not write myself, and I begged Wills to do so, because I regarded it as a simple act of conscientiousness, and wished it so to express itself. I am very sorry that we part company (though only in a literary sense), but I hope we shall work together again one day.

It has been blowing here to the most extraordinary extent. This morning is wonderfully bright and fine, but the weathercock points forever to the Sou' West.

Ever affec'ly,   C. D.

Gad's Hill Place, Higham by Rochester, Kent,
(Meaning Office),
Friday, Twenty-fourth January, 1862.

MY DEAR WILKIE,—I have read the story [*No Name*] as far as you have written it, with strong interest and great admiration.

As Wills petitions to read it before it comes back to you, and as I know you don't want it at once, *he* will very shortly return it to Harley Street.

I find in the book every quality that made the success of the *Woman in White*, without the least sign of holding on to that success or being taken in tow by it. I have no doubt whatever of the public reception of what I have read. You may be quite certain of it. I could not be more so than I am.

You will excuse my saying, with a reference to what is to follow, something that may be already in your own mind. It seems to me that great care is needed not to tell the story too severely. In exact proportion as you play around it here and there, and mitigate the severity of your own sticking to it, you will enhance and intensify the power with which Magdalen holds on to her purpose. For this reason I should have given Mr. Pendril some touches of comicality, and should have generally lighted up the house with some such capital touches of whimsicality and humour as those with

which you have irradiated the private the-
atricals.

This is the only suggestion in the critical
way that comes into my mind.   By-the-bye
—except one.   Look again to the scene
where Magdalen, in Mr. Pendril's presence
and that of Frank's father (who is excellent),
checks off the items of the position one by
one.   She strikes me as doing this in too
business-like and clerkly a way.

Wills clamours for the name, and that is
most difficult to find.   Here are some,
founded on more than one phase of the
book :

    (1) Below the Surface.   (Used.)
    (2) Under-Currents.   (Used.)
    (3) Through Thick and Thin.
    (4) Straight On.
    (5) Five Years' Work.
    (6) The Twig and the Tree.
    (7) The Blossom and the Fruit.
o (8) Behind the Veil.   1.
    (9) Secret Springs.
o (10) In Account with Michael Vanstone.
    (11) The Turning Point.
    (12) Lower and Lower.

(13) Latent Forces.
(14) Which is Which?
(15) Working in the Dark.
(16) One Purpose.
(17) Pitfalls.
(18) Changed, or Developed?
(19) The Vanstone Family.
(20) Magdalen Vanstone.
(21) Playing out the Play.
o (22) Nature's Own Daughter.   2
o (23) The Combe Raven Property.   4.
(24) Magdalen's Changes.
(25) Magdalen's Purpose.
(26) The Beginning and the End.   5.
(27) The Combe Raven Tragedy. ·

Gad's Hill Place,
Higham by Rochester, Kent,
Sunday, Twenty-seventh July, 1862.

MY DEAR WILKIE,—I shall be at Dover at half past 3 (as nearly as I—the punctual one —can calculate) next Monday (Monday) afternoon. Supposing I were to take a fly and come over to you until Wednesday morning, when the Forsters are coming here, might that suit your Book—literally as well as figuratively?

When I say "next Monday," I am an Ass.
I mean Monday the 4th of August.

Or could you do this!—Would you and
yours come over in a fly from Broadstairs
and dine with me at the Warden, and then
we would all go back to Broadstairs together?

Answer to the office, so that I may find
your note there on Wednesday morning
when I wake up. I will then arrange accordingly. Of course, if you are busy, you
will no more hesitate to say so to me than
I should, if I were writing a book, hesitate
to say so to you. . . .

Ever affectionately,   C. D.

No. 26, Wellington Street, Strand,
London, W. C.,
Saturday, Twentieth September, 1862.

MY DEAR WILKIE,—I have gone through
the Second Volume [*No Name*] at a sitting,
and I find it *wonderfully fine*. It goes on
with an ever-rising power and force in it that
fills me with admiration. It is as far before
and beyond *The Woman in White* as *that*
was beyond the wretched common level of
fiction-writing. There are some touches in

the Captain which no one but a born (and cultivated) writer could get near — could draw within hail of. And the originality of Mrs. Wragge, without compromise of her probability, involves a really great achievement. But they are all admirable ; Mr. Noel Vanstone and the housekeeper, both in their way as meritorious as the rest; Magdalen wrought out with truth, energy, sentiment, and passion, of the very first water.

I cannot tell you with what a strange dash of pride as well as pleasure I read the great results of your hard work. Because, as you know, I was certain from the *Basil* days that you were the Writer who would come ahead of all the Field—being the only one who combined invention and power, both humourous and pathetic, with that invincible determination to work, and that profound conviction that nothing of worth is to be done without work, of which triflers and feigners have no conception.

I send the books back, by South Eastern Railway to-day.

There is one slight slip, occurring more

than once, which you have not corrected. Magdalen "laid down," and I think some one else "laid down." It is clear that she must either lay herself down, or lie down. To lay is a verb active, and to lie down is a verb neuter, consequently she lay down, or laid herself down.

It would be a very great pleasure to me if I could get to you once again at Broad-stairs, but I fear it is not at all likely. I forget how long you stay there. Will you tell me? We propose going to Paris on the 20th of October. I have half a mind to read in Paris when I *am* there; but this is as yet an unformed object in my thoughts.

You will not be able, I suppose, to do any little thing for the Xmas No.? I have done the introduction and conclusion, and will send them you by-and-bye, when the Printer shall have (Thos. Wills) "dealt with them." They are done in the character of a Waiter, and I think are very droll. The leading idea admits of any kind of contribution, and does not require it to be in any way whatever accounted for. Besides having this advantage, it is a comic defiance of the difficulty of a

Xmas No., with an unexpected end to it.
The name (between ourselves) is *Somebody's
Luggage.* ...

> Ever, dear Wilkie,
> > Affectionately yours,   C. D.

No. 26, Wellington Street, Strand,
London, W. C.,
Saturday, Fourth October, 1862.

MY DEAR WILKIE,—I write very hastily
before going up to see the horrid Poole
(who's ill), and then going home to Gad's.
Enclosed are the first and last papers of the
Xmas No.   You will understand that the
titles will be something like this :

SOMEBODY'S LUGGAGE.

His Leaving it till Called for.
His Portmanteau.
His Desk.
His Boots.
His Collar-Box.
His Brown Paper Parcels.
His Dressing-Case.
His Umbrella.
His Wonderful End.

8

I am doing a little French story for it, which reproduces (I think, to the life) the ways and means of a dull fortified French town, full of French soldiers. . . .

Ever affec'ly,   C. D.

No. 26, Wellington Street, Strand,
London, W. C.,
Wednesday, Eighth October, 1862.

MY DEAR WILKIE,—I am really quite concerned that you should have bothered your sufficiently occupied mind about the Xmas No. Of course it seems very strange and bare to me not to have you in it; but I never seriously contemplated the reasonable likelihood of your being able to do anything for it.

It is a great pleasure to me that you like the notion (and execution) so well. The difficulty of carrying out your suggestion is this: it would destroy a good deal of the effect of the end—*His Wonderful End*—and does not at present seem to me quite reconcilable with it as a piece of execution. But I will turn it over again.

I have done a little story for *His Boots*, very slight in itself, but into which I have tried to infuse (fancifully) every conceivable feature of an old fortified French town. It is very like, I think. When I have the proof I will send it you to read at any odd times. I think I shall now go at some short odd comic notion, to supply your place. I am bent upon making a good No. to go with *No Name*. . . .

Macready was with us from last Saturday to Monday. Very little altered indeed—and with not the end of one single sentence within 450 miles of him.

Of course I will report myself in Paris before we have been there many days (we start on Sunday week), and give you my address as soon as I have such a thing to my back. I am not going to have any establishment there, but intend the dinner to be brought in on a man's shoulders (you know the tray) from a Restaurant.

I saw Poole (for my sins) last Saturday, and he *was* a sight. He had got out of bed to receive me (at 3 P.M.) and tried to look as if he had been up at Dawn—with a dirty and obviously warm impression of himself on the bedclothes. It was a tent bedstead with four wholly unaccounted for and bare

poles, each with an immense spike on the
top, like four Lightning conductors. He had
a fortnight's grey beard, and had made a
lot of the most extraordinary memoranda
of questions to ask me—which he couldn't
read—through an eyeglass which he couldn't
hold. He was continually beset with a notion that his landlady was listening outside
the door, and was continually getting up from
a kind of ironing-board at which he sat, with
the intention of darting at the door, but invariably missed his aim, and brought himself up by the forehead against blind cor-
ners of the wall. He had a dressing-gown
over his night-shirt, and wore his trousers
where Blondin wears his Baskets. He said,
with the greatest indignation, I might suppose what sort of "society" he could get
out of his landlady, when he mentioned that
she could say nothing, on being consulted
by him touching the Poison-case at the old
Bailey, but "People didn't ought to poison
people, sir ; its wrong."

Ever affec'ly,   C. D.

Gad's Hill Place,
Higham by Rochester, Kent,
Tuesday, Fourteenth October, 1862.

MY DEAR WILKIE, — I have read those proofs carefully [*No Name*]. They are very strong indeed.

I am not sure that I quite understand within what limitations you want my opinion of them. The only points that strike me as at all questionable are all details. But not to pass them over, here they are.

I find Mrs. Lecount's proceeding with the new will rather violently sudden, followed, as it is so immediately, by the death. Also, I do not quite like her referring to those drafts she has brought with her. It would be so very suspicious in the eyes of a suspicious man.

I forget whether you want that Laudanum bottle again. If not, I think Mrs. Lecount should break it before Noel Vanstone's eyes. Otherwise, while he is impressed with the danger he supposes himself to have escaped, he repeats it, on a smaller scale, by giving Mrs. Lecount an inducement to kill him, and leaving the means at hand.

I believe it would be *necessary* for a Testator signing his will to inform the witnesses of the fact of its being his will—though of its contents, of course, they would be ignorant. The legal form of attestation in use is: Signed, sealed, and delivered by so and so, the written named Testator, *as and for his last will and testament,* in the presence of us, etc.

If the story were mine I should decidedly not put into it the anticipation contained in the last line or two of Norah's postscript. But that is a moot point in art.

Throughout the whole of the thirty-sixth weekly part is there wanting some sense on the part of Noel Vanstone that he may not be legally married at all? This seems to me the most important question.

I do not quite follow the discussion between Noel and Lecount about the eight months' interval, and the puzzling of Magdalen by taking that number. Why? Mrs. Lecount says, "People easily guess a year; people easily guess six months." Suppose she did guess six months, she would only have to bestir herself so much the more.

And it is clear that a plotter, bent upon losing no chance, would take the shortest likely time and not the longest.   Then what is gained by eight?

Among the many excellent things in the proof, I noticed, as particularly admirable, the manner in which the amount of Mrs. Lecount's legacy is got at, and the bearing and discourse of the Scotch fly-driver.

I break off hastily to get this into the box before it is cleared at the gate here.   From Paris I will write again.   My address there until further notice Hotel Meurice.

Ever affec'ly,   C. D.

A second letter from Dickens to Collins written later on the same day, October 14th, and already published by Miss Hogarth and Miss Dickens in their Collection, is given here in part, as showing the thoughtful kindness and sympathy of the writer, and his willingness to give his own time and labor, so valuable to him then as a working man of letters, to help a friend in distress.

Gad's Hill Place,
Higham by Rochester, Kent,
Tuesday Night, October 14th, 1862.

MY DEAR WILKIE,—Frank Beard has been here this evening, of course since I posted my this day's letter to you, and has told me that you are not at all well, and how he has given you something which he hopes and believes will bring you round.   It is not to convey this insignificant piece of intelligence, or to tell you how anxious I am that you should come up with a wet sheet and a flowing sail (as we say at sea when we are not sick), that I write.   It is simply to say what follows, which I hope may save you some mental uneasiness — for I was stricken ill when I was doing *Bleak House*, and I shall not easily forget what I suffered under the fear of not being able to come up to time.   Dismiss that fear (if you have it) altogether from your mind. Write to me at Paris at any moment, and say you are unequal to your work, and want me, and I will come to London straight, and do your work.   I am quite confident that, with your notes, and a few words of explanation, I could take it up at any time and do it. Absurdly unnecessary to say that it would be a makeshift! But I could do it, at a pinch, so like you as that no one should find out the difference. Don't make much of this offer in your mind; it is nothing except to ease it. If you should want help, I am as safe as the bank. The trouble will be nothing to me, and the triumph of overcoming a difficulty great. Think it a Christmas Number, an *Idle Apprentice*, a *Lighthouse*, a *Frozen Deep*. I am as ready as in any of these cases to strike in and hammer the iron out.

You won't want me. You will be well (and thankless) in no time. But there I am; and I hope that the knowledge may be a comfort to you. Call me and I come.

> Gad's Hill Place,
> Higham by Rochester, Kent,
> New Year's Day, 1863.

My DEAR WILKIE,—Many thanks for the book [*No Name*], the arrival of which has created an immense sensation in this palatial abode. I am delighted (but not surprised) to hear of its wonderful sale; all that I thought and said of it when you finished the second volume, I think and repeat of it now you have finished the third.

On Thursday in next week I shall certainly be at the office; and I shall sleep there on that night, and on the Friday, and on the Saturday. On the Sunday I vanish into space for a day or two; but I must be in Paris about Thursday the 15th, because on Saturday the 17th I am going to read Copperfield gratuitously at the Embassy.

Will you dine at the office on Thursday in next week, at 6?

Let me strongly advise you to "go in" now for getting thoroughly set up and made well. Don't do it by halves, but go through with it and see it out. Are there no baths that would drive the rheumatic Devil out of that game leg? Who knows but that towards the end of February I might be open to any foreign proposal whatsoever? Distance no object, climate of no importance, change the advertiser's motive.

All the good wishes of the day and year, from   Yours ever affec'ly,   C. D.

Paris, Hotel du Helder,
Thursday, January Twenty-ninth, 1863.

MY DEAR WILKIE,—I came back here yesterday, and was truly concerned to read your poor account of yourself. . . .

According to my present knowledge, I shall be here until next Wednesday morning. I may be here a day later, but cannot positively say at this moment. Of course, if you come over before I go, you will let me know immediately. If you could not get such a look-out as you want at the Louvre, I think you would be sure to get it at the Grand Hotel—the new monster, belonging (I think) to the same company. Its situation on the Boulevard, just at the head of the Rue de la Paix, I should prefer for an Invalid. Nothing can be more cheerful.

You will be interested in knowing that Paris is immeasurably more wicked than ever. The time of the Regency seems restored, and "Long Live the Devil" seems the social motto.

I read to-night and to-morrow—horribly against the grain as the grain is at present; but I suppose it will be kinder towards night. I went down to my room to rehearse this morning (a thing I never did in my life before, but I have not read Dombey these twelve months), and I feel as if I could not muster spirits and composure enough to get through the child's death.

John has *no* British prejudices—a very remarkable phenomenon in a man in his station in life, unacquainted with the language, and left here for a week to subsist wholly on Pantomime.

Ever affectionately,   C. D.

Gad's Hill Place,
Higham by Rochester, Kent,
Sunday, Twenty-eighth June, 1863.

MY DEAR WILKIE,—Welcome home! I heartily desire to see you, and hope you will soon be well enough (if you are not already) to come down here for those quiet days you wrote of from Germany.

I want to hear everything about you—whether you are as strong as you ought to be; whether the Baths bore out the Doctor; whether you are going again to Caplin [proprietor of an establishment devoted to medical baths] (whom I discover to be my dearest friend and brother); whether you set up your own Perambulator in that queer place yonder—if so, whether you doubled it up too—and all sorts of things.

Here am I with a swelling on the back of my head, and an itching—not palm, but neck. I cannot think the swelling was meant for me, and conceive that it *must* be a mistake. Macready was to have been here to-day, but is stopped at Cheltenham by (I can't write it) erysipelas. I am rather anxious about him, though his good wife writes very cheerfully.

We shall be at the office on Friday. Are you well enough to dine there at 5, and go afterwards to the German Reed's? I am told that [John] Parry is doing the most amusing thing of its kind that ever was done. If you could come, I would write to Priscilla [Mrs. Reed] for stalls. Give me a word in answer by return here.

Ever affectionately,   C. D.

Gad's Hill Place,
Higham, by Rochester, Kent,
Sunday, Ninth August, 1863,

MY DEAR WILKIE,— Although your account of yourself is not so brilliant as I had hoped you might be able to render by this time, I rejoice to hear from you to any effect. I had divined that you had discovered a yacht and gone on a cruise, and did not wonder at your going as soon as you could. Your plan for the winter is the best you could make, I think. I hope nôthing will prevent your coming here, as you propose, for a little while before you depart.

It is extremely hot here—so very hot today that I retired to my bedroom (from which I write) after lunch, and reduced myself to my shirt and drawers. In that elegant costume I achieve the present feat of penmanship. The De la Rues, of Genoa, are coming to England; I expect them here for three days this next week. . . .

I am always thinking of writing a long book, and am never beginning to do it. I have not been anywhere for ever and ever so long, but am thinking of evaporating for a fortnight on the 18th. . . .

All send love.   Ever, my dear Wilkie,
         Affec'ly yours,   C. D.

No. 26 Wellington Street, Strand,
London, W. C.,
Thursday, Twenty-fourth September, 1863.

MY DEAR WILKIE,—I hope the abominable gout, having shewn itself in time, will not detain you in this climate long.   It is beyond all doubt in my mind that the best thing you can do is to get off.

The Girders* were both got up by 8 o'clock at night.   It was ticklish work—nine men gasping, snuffling, heaving, snorting, balancing themselves on bricks, and tumbling over each other.   But it really was well done, and with great cheerfulness and spirit, to which three gallons of beer, judiciously thrown in, imparted a festive air.

Nothing has fallen down or blown up since.   Yawning chasms abound, and dust

[* Iron girders at Gad's Hill, which were necessitated by adding another room to the drawing-room of the house.]

obscures all objects ; but we hope to weather it.

I shall be anxious to hear how the gout gets on.   Ever affec'ly,   C. D.

P. S.—Two little men, who did nothing, made a show of doing it all, and drank one gallon of the beer.

Collins spent the winter of 1863–64 in Italy, and, as already published in *The Letters*, Dickens wrote to him on January 24th from Gad's Hill, as follows :

"The Christmas Number [*Mrs. Lirriper's Lodgings*] has been the greatest success of all ; has shot ahead of last year ; has sold about two hundred and twenty thousand ; and has made the name of Mrs. Lirriper so swiftly and domestically famous as never was. I had a very strong belief in her when I wrote about her, finding that she made a great effect upon me ; but she certainly has gone beyond my hope. (Probably you know nothing about her ? which is a very unpleasant consideration.) Of the new book [*Our Mutual Friend*] I have done the first two numbers, and am now beginning the third. It is a combination of drollery with romance which requires a great deal of pains and a perfect throwing away of points that might be amplified; but I hope it is *very good*. . . . You will have read about poor Thackeray's death—sudden, and yet not sudden, for he had long been alarmingly ill. At the solicitation of Mr. Smith and some of his friends, I have done what I would most gladly have excused myself from doing—if I felt I could—written a couple of pages about him in what was his own magazine."

Gad's Hill Place,
Higham by Rochester, Kent,
Wednesday, Tenth January, 1866.

MY DEAR WILKIE,—Proofs, Proofs, Proofs! where are the *Armadale* proofs I was to have? O where, and O where!—&c.

If, in the remote dark coming ages, when you shall have done this book, you would care to come back to the old quarters—not for such another labor thereawhile, but for Idle Apprentices and such like Wanderings with the Inimitable Undersigned—always

9

remember that Wills with carte blanche, and I with open arms, await you.

Ever affect'ly,   C. D.

Gad's Hill Place,
Higham by Rochester, Kent,
Tuesday, Ninth July, 1866.

MY DEAR WILKIE,—I have gone through the play [a dramatization of *Armadale*] very carefully. The plot is extraordinarily got together; its compactness is quite amazing; and the dialogue is very excellent in all the rare essentials of being terse, witty, characteristic, and dramatic.

But insuperable and ineradicable from the whole piece is—*Danger*. Almost every situation in it is dangerous. I do not think any English audience would accept the Scene in which Miss Gwilt in that Widow's dress renounces Midwinter. And if you got so far, you would never get through the last act in the Sanatorium. You could only carry those situations on a real hard wooden stage, and wrought out (very indifferently) by real live people face to face with other real live people judging them — you could only carry those situations *by the help of interest in some innocent person whom they placed in peril, and that person a young woman.* There is no one to be interested in here. Let who will play Midwinter, the saving interest cannot be got out of him. There is no relief from the wickedness of the rest; and in exact proportion to the skilful heaping up of it the danger accumulates.

I know as well as you do that this is merely one man's opinion. But I so strongly entertain the opinion that the odds are heavily against an audience's seeing the play out that I should not be your friend if I blinked it. I see the piece before me on the stage. Then I change my point of view, and act Midwinter, and act Miss Gwilt. A perfect terror of the difficult and dangerous ground oppresses me in both positions, and I feel my inability to carry the situations myself as strongly as I feel the inability of any professed actor or actress alive to carry them for me.

In reference to your two questions, I have no doubt whatever as to the first—that the substitution of the Manuscript for the marked printed pages is a decided improvement.

As to the second, I think that any advantage to be gained from acting those events instead of narrating them would be more than counterbalanced by lengthening the play. They don't take long to tell, as they stand, and seem quite clear. Again, I think they would be much more difficult to act than to narrate. . . .

I will send the play-book to you to-morrow by the hands of one of the office people. Next week I purpose being at the office on Saturday at 1. At ten minutes past 2 on the said Saturday in next week I purpose coming down here. Can you come with me?

Ever affectionately,   C. D.

No. 26, Wellington Street, Strand,
London, W. C.,
Thursday, Fourth October, 1866.

MY DEAR WILKIE,—None of the scenery was painted over, but it was cut down into small panels for the decoration of the Theatre Rooms in Tavistock House. Those canvases still exist in Chapman and Hall's warehouse, where they are carefully preserved. But they are so separated from their contexts (so to speak), and are, for stage purposes, so unintelligible—being small bits of complicated sets—that I think they would put the Olympic painter into chains instead of helping him. Moreover, it would be hardly fair to the dear old boy who painted them to reproduce them for such a purpose, at such a disadvantage.

If your memory fails you anywhere as to the position of any practicable parts of the Scenery on which " Business " depends, I have no doubt I can jog it.

Retain your last faith. Trust my stomach as an Institution superior to the cavils of scepticism.

This is a pretty state of things! That I should be in Christmas Labour [*Mugby Junction*] while you are cruising about the world, a compound of Hayward and Captain Cook! But I am so undoubtedly one of the sons of Toil—and fathers of children —that I expect to be presently presented with a smock frock, a pair of leather breeches, and a pewter watch, for having brought up the largest family ever known. . . .

Ever affectionately,   C. D.

Dickens's Readings in England for a number of years were under the management of the Messrs. Chappell, of Bond Street, London. They paid all of his expenses, and gave him at first £50 a night, later £60, and finally £80, and in two years they paid him £13,000, besides the £20,000 he made in America.

Dickens was a passenger on the train derailed at Staplehurst, June 9, 1865, with great loss of life; he never fully recovered from the shock to his nerves, and, strangely enough, he died on the 9th of June, five years later.

Griffith Gaunt, first published in 1866, excited no little adverse criticism on both sides of the Atlantic — criticism which inspired *The Prurient Prude*, one of Charles Reade's most characteristic performances. Dickens was not called upon to testify in public concerning his views of the novel, but Reade brought suit for libel against the proprietors of *The Round Table*, an American publication, and by an intelligent jury of his peers he was awarded pecuniary damages to the amount of six American cents.

Office, Tuesday, Twelfth February, 1867.

MY DEAR WILKIE,—Coming back here yesterday I found your letter awaiting me.

Owing to my heavy engagements I have not read Charles Reade's last book, but I will take it away with me to-morrow, and do so at once. If the trial should come off in this present month, however, I *cannot* be a witness; for I go to Scotland to-morrow, and come back for only one night at St. James's Hall before going to Ireland. The public announcements are all made, and heavy expenses are incurred by Chappell, wherefore I must be producible, in common honor. But I hope the action may not be tried so soon. I do not agree with the legal authorities, and I rather doubt Cockburn's allowing such evidence to be given on the ground that the *onus probandi* lies with the reviewer, and that it is not disproof that is required — but this is beside the question. Say everything that is brotherly in art from me to Reade, and add that I will write to you again after having got through the story.

I am as fresh as can possibly be expected under the work of the Readings. But the railways shake me, as witness my present handwriting. Since the Staplehurst experience I feel them very much.

This day fortnight I shall be at St. James's
Hall in the evening, and perhaps we can then
have a word together — unless you are in
Paris by that time.

Ever affec'ly,   C. D.

Bridge of Allan, Scotland,
Wednesday, Twentieth February, 1867.

My dear Wilkie,—I have read Charles
Reade's book, and here follows my state of
mind—*as a witness*—respecting it.

I have read it with the strongest interest
and admiration.   I regard it as the work of a
highly accomplished writer and a good man ;
a writer with a brilliant fancy and a grace-
ful and tender imagination.   I could name
no other living writer who could, in my opinion, write such a story nearly so well.   As
regards a so-called critic who should decry
such a book as Hollywell Street literature,
and the like, I should have merely to say of
him that I could desire no stronger proof of
his incapacity in, and his unfitness for, the
post to which he has elected himself.

Cross-examined, I should feel myself in
danger of being put on unsafe ground, and

should try to set my wits against the cross-examiner, to keep well off it. But if I were reminded (as I probably should be, suppos-ing the evidence to be allowed at all) that I was the Editor of a periodical of large cir-culation in which the Plaintiff himself had written, and if I had [had] read to me in court those passages about Gaunt's going up to his wife's bed drunk and that last child's being conceived, and was asked whether, as Editor, I would have passed those passages, whether written by the Plaintiff or anybody else, I should be obliged to reply No. Asked why? I should say that what was pure to an artist might be impurely suggestive to inferior minds (of which there must neces-sarily be many among a large mass of read-ers), and that I should have called the writer's attention to the likelihood of those passages being perverted in such quarters. Asked if I should have passed the passage where Kate and Mary have the illegitimate child upon their laps and look over its little points together? I should be again obliged to re-ply No, for the same reason. Asked wheth-er, as author or Editor, I should have passed

Neville's marriage to Mercy, and should have placed those four people, Gaunt, his wife, Mercy, and Neville, in those relative situations towards one another, I should again be obliged to reply No. Hard pressed upon this point, I must infallibly say that I consider those relative situations extremely coarse and disagreeable.

I am staying in this quiet, pretty place for a day and a half, to recruit a little. To-morrow night I am in Glasgow again, and on Friday and Saturday in Edinburgh (Graham's Hotel, Prince's Street). Then I turn homeward for Tuesday night at St. James's Hall. Enormous crowds everywhere.

Affectionately ever,   C. D.

Gad's Hill Place,
Higham by Rochester, Kent,
Office, Thirteenth March, 1867.

My dear Wilkie,—By all means let Reade see my letter.

This from a disconsolate Voyager with the Fenians before him. I should as soon have thought of going to Ireland at this time, out of my own head, as of going to read at—what was its name in those geological periods when you sprained your foot?—Aspatria. But Chappell's head thinks differently.

Glad to hear of our friend Regnier [of the Théâtre Français]. As Carlyle would put it: "A deft and shifty little man, brisk and sudden, of a most ingenious carpentering faculty, and not without constructive qualities of a higher than the Beaver sort. Withal an actor, though of a somewhat hard tone. Think pleasantly of him, O ye children of men!"

Ever UnPatrick-iotically,   C. D.

No Thoroughfare was the last of the Christmas stories. It was written by Dickens and Collins, each contributing an equal part; and it appeared, in 1867, in the holiday number of *All the Year Round*.

Stoke-upon-Trent,
Wednesday, First May, 1867.

MY DEAR WILKIE,—Of course I know nothing of your arrangements when I ask you the following question:

Would you like to do the next Xmas No. with me—we two alone, each taking half?

Of course I assume that the money question is satisfactorily disposed of between you and Wills. Equally, of course, I suppose our two names to be appended to the performance.

I put this to you, I need hardly say, before having in any way approached the subject in my own mind as to contrivance, character, story, or anything else.

To-morrow night at Warrington will finish my present course—with the exception of one night at Croydon, and one more night at St. James's Hall, which I count as nothing. I shall be at Gad's from Saturday to Monday, inclusive. After that either Gad's or the office will soon find me.

Ever affectionately,   C. D.

Gad's Hill Place,
Higham by Rochester, Kent,
Tuesday, Second July, 1867.

THIS is to certify that I, the undersigned, was (for the time being) a drivelling ass when I declared the Christmas Number to be composed of Thirty-two pages. And I do hereby declare that the said Christmas Number is composed of Forty-eight pages, and long and heavy pages too, as I have heretofore proved and demonstrated with the sweat of my brow. (Signed) CHARLES DICKENS.

Witness to the signature of the said Charles Dickens :   BUMBLE (Puppy).

Gad's Hill Place,
Higham by Rochester, Kent,
Friday, Twenty-third August, 1867.

MY DEAR WILKIE,—I have done the over-ture, but I don't write to make *that* feeble report.

I have a general idea which I hope will supply the kind of interest we want. Let us arrange to culminate in a wintry flight and pursuit across the Alps, under lonely circum-stances, and against warnings. Let us get into all the horrors and dangers of such an adventure under the most terrific circum-stances, either escaping from or trying to overtake (the latter, the latter, I think) some one, on escaping from or overtaking whom the love, prosperity, and Nemesis of the story depend. There we can get Ghostly interest, picturesque interest, breathless in-terest of time and circumstance, and force the design up to any powerful climax we please. If you will keep this in your mind as I will in mine, urging the story towards it as we go along, we shall get a very Avalanche of power out of it, and thunder it down on the readers' heads.

Ever affec'ly,   C. D.

Gad's Hill Place,
Higham by Rochester, Kent,
Monday, Ninth September, 1867.

MY DEAR WILKIE,—This note requires no answer, and is merely thrown out to be taken up into your meditations.

Q'ry: whether we require any money fraud rom Obenreizer after all? Whether his best fraud may not be, after discovering Vendale to be the real man (*a disappointment to him* as he hoped to do him an injury, not a service), to resolve to set himself up as the real man, and to put Vendale out of the way forever? Q'ry: whether this, and his resolve to destroy some proof along with Vendale, is not the best fraud for the story?

I am so bringing him out, as that he may go with either this design or the other.

Also, I have made Vendale formerly in
the Counting House with Wilding, so that
they have previous acquaintance with, and
confidence in, one another, when we bring
them together. This makes the opening of
the chapter, "The New Partner Acts," far
more natural, and makes the way quite easy
for Wilding's will.

Ever affec'ly,   C. D.

Gad's Hill Place,
Higham by Rochester, Kent,
Tuesday, Tenth September, 1867.

MY DEAR WILKIE,—Odd that we should
be moved to write cross letters !

Let us meet at the office at $\frac{1}{2}$ past 12
on *Friday.* I don't think I shall have done
Wilding's death by that time (I have been
steadily at work, but slowly, laying ground);
but the Obenreizer-reproduction chapter will
be ready to run over. All the points you
dwell upon are already in it.

It will be an immense point if we can arrange to *start you for a long run, beginning
immediately after Wilding's death,* and if I
can at the same time be told off to come in,

while you are at work, with the Alpine as
cent and adventures. *Then*, in two or three
days of writing together, we could finish. I
am very anxious to finish, my mind being so
distracted by America, and the interval so
short.

Reverting to my proposed appointment
for Friday, let me add that if you are free I
could dine with you at the Athenæum on
Thursday, at ¼ past 5, if you would undertake to order dinner. This would give us
more time. But perhaps you are engaged?

*If Thursday be our appointment, write by
return.* If Friday, don't write.

Ever affec'ly,   C. D.

Kind regards to your mother.

Have you done—or are you doing—the
beginning of the chapter "Exit Wilding"?
I shall very soon want it.

Collins during this year was contributing
to *All the Year Round* his novel called *The
Moonstone*, concerning which Dickens wrote
to Wills :

"I have read the first three numbers of
Wilkie's story this morning [June 13, 1867],

and have gone minutely through the plot of the rest to the last line. It gives a series of 'narratives,' but it is a very curious story, wild, and yet domestic, with excellent character in it, and great mystery. It is prepared with extraordinary care, and has every chance of being a hit. It is in many respects much better than anything he has done."

No. 26, Wellington Street, Strand,
London, W. C.
Wednesday, Eighteenth September, 1867.

MY DEAR WILKIE,—Frederick Chapman came here yesterday. After some preparatory references to his own contracts and engagements (which were true), he asked me if he might enter on the question of your copyrights, in partnership with Smith and Son. As nothing could be better for your books than that they should fall into Smith's hands, I graciously replied yes. It then appeared that he had seen Smith, who was "disposed to go into the matter," and who evidently had expressed an opinion that it might be brought to bear. Thereupon I dictated to F. C.—for him to write down—

10

the general purport of your memorandum, wherewith he is to hold conference with Smith before coming back to me. He expressed an opinion that Smith and Elder's demand was very high.

As he asked me whether he might except the new story here [*The Moonstone*] for himself to offer for, and as I don't think you would make as good terms for it in the batch as separately, I again graciously said yes.

I am jogging on (at the pace of a wheelbarrow propelled by a Greenwich Pensioner) at the doomed Wilding.

Ever affec'ly,   C. D.

Before Dickens sailed for his second American visit, in November, 1867, with George Dolby as his business agent, he gave Collins some assistance in making a stage version of *No Thoroughfare* for Fechter. This is the only one of Dickens's works in the dramatization of which he had any hand, except *The Tale of Two Cities*, the production of which at the Lyceum, under the management of Madame ·Céleste in 1860, he supervised and superintended. Fechter made a great success in the part of Obenrei-

zer, in London, in the winter of 1867–68, and
later in Paris, and in the United States. Mr.
William J. Florence was the original Obenreizer in this country. Mr. Lawrence Barrett,
learning that he could not control the American rights to the drama, never attempted to
produce it.

Gad's Hill Place,
Higham by Rochester, Kent,
Monday, Twenty-third September, 1867.

MY DEAR WILKIE,—Like you I am working with snail-like slowness. My American
possibility divides my mind so incongruous-
ly with this occupation.

But I think I have a good idea. I send it
you with a view to your at odd times Think-
ing-out of the last Act. When Vendale is
at the last pass of the murderous business
on the Simplon, he conscientiously says
some broken words to Obenreizer to the
effect: "If it be possible that you are *the
man*—as I have lately thought—do so and
so. Villain and murderer as you are, my
trust to my dead friend remains unchang-
ed." This is so brokenly said that Obenreizer supposes it refers to some obscurity

in Vendale's birth — not his own — and so goes on to build up Nemesis.

I have already got Vendale haunted by the possibility that Obenreizer *is* the man.

I will write again by or before Friday. I see a great chance for Act III. out of this leaving of Act II. Don't you?

Ever affec'ly,   C. D.

The Demon Illegibility has possession of me.

Gad's Hill Place,
Higham by Rochester, Kent,
Saturday, Fifth October, 1867.

MY DEAR WILKIE, — I have brought on Marguerite to the rescue, and I have so left it as that Vendale — to spare her — says it was an accident in the storm and nothing more. By the way, Obenreizer has received a cut from Vendale, made with his own dagger. This in case you want him with a scar. If you don't, no matter.

I have no doubt my Proof of the Mountain adventure will be full of mistakes, as my MS. is not very legible. But you will see what it means.

The Denouement I see pretty much as

you see it—without further glimpses as yet. The Obenreizer question I will consider (q'ry, Suicide?). I have made Marguerite wholly devoted to her lover.

Whenever you may give me notice of your being ready, we will appoint to meet here to wind up.

I don't go until the ninth of November, the *Scotia* being full. I have an officer's cabin on deck in the steamer.

Affec'ly ever, C. D.

No. 26, Wellington Street, Strand,
London, W. C.,
Wednesday, Ninth October, 1867.

MY DEAR WILKIE,—Will you notice in the chapter "Vendale Writes a Letter," that we are in some danger of making him rather foolish or contemptible in the eyes of readers by being so blind to the fact that Obenreizer *is* the man? A very slight alteration or two will remove the objection. I suggest that it should not then be quite so plain, even to the reader, that Obenreizer *is* the man; and that when Vendale might be on the verge of supposing him to be the man,

Obenreizer should disarm him by some skilful reference to Marguerite. Make it, in fact, a part of Vendale's fidelity to Marguerite that he should not connect the theft and forgery with Obenreizer.

I am racking my brains for a good death to that respectable gentleman.

Ever affec'ly,　　C. D.

Parker House, Boston, U. S.,
Thursday, Twenty-eighth November, 1867.

MY DEAR WILKIE,—I have received a letter from one Mr. Barrett, an American actor (dated 308 Regent Street, London, W.), proposing for the dramatic version of *No Thoroughfare*. He says in that letter that he "learns from Mr. Wilkie Collins that I have taken the play to America, intending to arrange for its production there," and offers to come out here with the New Year and play it. As I have not got the play, I am at a loss to know whether this is an intentional or an unintentional mistake.

Now, Dolby is going over to New York this morning, and has it in charge from me to see the most speculative of dramatic men there, and ascertain what terms he will make for the Play. I think it far better to deal with a man here than with a man in Regent Street, London. The excitement in New York about the Readings being represented as quite unprecedented, I have little doubt of being able to make a good thing of the Drama, and, if necessary, I will get it up. But what I shall want *as soon as I can possibly have them*, are :

1. A detailed Scene Plot from Fechter.

2. His notion of the Dresses.

3. A copy of the Play itself, Act by Act, as you do it.

4. Together with any stage Directions that Fechter has in his mind.

Thus armed, I should not be at all surprised if I could get a very handsome addition to our gains. I think it will be worth while for you, on receipt of this, to telegraph to me at the Westminster Hotel, Irving Place, New York City, *when* you will be able to send me *the last of the Play*, because I shall then be in a condition to make a contract. Tell Fechter, with my love and regards, that I will write him a note immediately after my first Reading here next Monday. (Between ourselves, I have already some £2000 in hand before opening my lips.)

I am yearning already for the Spring and Home, but hope to work out the intervening time with a tolerably stout heart. I am wonderfully well in health, and got over the voyage with the greatest success.

This note is left open for Dolby to add Postscript to. He will know, before closing it, whether or no it is certainly worth while for you to telegraph (in 20 words, containing not more than 100 letters). It will be best for you always to address me about the Play, and always to address whatever you send in connection with it, Westminster Hotel, Irving Place, New York City.

Ever, my dear Wilkie, your affectionate
                    CHARLES DICKENS.

I will not at present reply to Mr. Barrett at all.

                    Westminster Hotel,
              New York, 29 Nov., 1867.

MY DEAR MR. COLLINS,—I have only time —to save the Mail—to add a few lines to

Mr. Dickens's letter to request you will send out the acting part of the Play as soon as possible, as I am in hopes I may be able to arrange for its production here, possibly at Wallack's; and if you can get models made and sent out of the Scenery, it will also be a great thing to have.   I spoke to [Harry] Palmer about the price last evening on my arrival here, and he seems most enthusiastic on the matter.

I have sold to-day the tickets for the first Four Readings in the City, and sold out (8000 tickets in all) in six hours.   The enthusiasm with regard to Dickens and all that he does is enormous, and I am in hopes we shall be able to spend the whole of our t'me in the large cities.

Give my kindest regards to Wills and all London friends, and believe me,

Yours faithfully,   GEORGE DOLBY.

Parker House, Boston,
Monday, Second December, 1867.

MY DEAR WILKIE,—I find that *if the Play be left unpublished in England*, the right of playing it in America can be secured by as-

signing the MS. to an American Citizen.
That I can do at once by using my publishers here for the purpose. I can make an
arrangement with [Lester] Wallack, in New
York, to have it produced at his Theatre
(where there is the best company), on a
sharing agreement after a certain nightly al-
lowance for expenses, and I have arranged
to see Wallack next week.

I have made inquiry about Mr. Lawrence
Barrett (whose letter to me I enclose), and I
find that he has a good reputation as a Star
Actor, and that he is a responsible man pe-
cuniarily. Now, I am advised that the best
course will be to make an engagement with
him to take the play and act in it, and get
it up wheresoever he likes in the United
States, *except in New York City*. (The exception, because Wallack and he are not
d'accord, and the other good New York The-
atres all have their hands full.) As I read
his letter his proposal means that we give
the play—that he gives his services—and
that the *receipts* of each night's performance
be divided between author and actor equally. Will you write to him at once, see him,

and bind us both to such an engagement, if he be willing to bind himself to it? We might possibly get a good round sum by such a course. I have advised with one of the most knowing Managers in New York (who came over here this morning to see me)— the *Black Crook* Manager—and he says: "If you have Wallack for New York, and Barrett for the States generally, you could not do better." Mr. Barrett may have left England before this reaches you. If so, I have taken measures to catch [him] on this side when he comes over.

As I read for the first time to-night, I will finish this to-morrow for Wednesday's steamer, which will be my own *Cuba* returning.

Tuesday, Third December.

A most tremendous success last night. The whole city is perfectly mad about it to-day, and it is quite impossible that prospects could be more brilliant.

Ever, my dear Wilkie,

Your always affectionate   C. D.

Boston,
Christmas Eve, 1867.

MY DEAR WILKIE,—I am obliged to write very hastily, to catch the mail over at New York.

The Play is done *with great pains and skill*, but I fear it is too long.   Its fate will have been decided before you get this letter, but I greatly doubt its success.

Your points follow in their order.

1. Whatever is most dramatic in such a complicated thing as the Clock Lock I think the best for the stage, without reference to the nicety of the real mechanism.

2. I would keep Vendale and Marguerite on the stage, and I would end with Obenreizer's exit.

3. Madame D'Or's speaking unquestionably better out.   She herself unquestionably better out.   I have not the least doubt of it.

But, my dear boy, what do you mean by the whole thing being left "at my sole discretion"?   Is not the play coming out the day after to-morrow? ? ?

There are no end of *No Thoroughfares* being offered to Managers here.   The play being still in abeyance with Wallack, I have a strong suspicion that he wants to tide over to the 27th, and get a Telegram from London about the first night of the real version. If it should not be a great success, he would then either do a false one, or do none. Accordingly, I have brought him to book for decision on the 26th.   Don't you see?

They are doing *Cricket*, *Oliver Twist*, and all sorts of versions of me.   Under these circumstances they fence when they have to pay.

I will try to catch the next mail.

Ever affectionately,   C. D.

Philadelphia,
Thirty-first January, 1868.

MY DEAR WILKIE, — Your letter, dated on the 11th, reached me here this morning. Mine will be brief, as it must go on to New York presently, and there is much snow on the Line.

I am indeed delighted by your account of the Play, and do begin to believe that I shall see it!   Every word of your account of your last visit " Behind" I have read—and shall read—again and again.

Of Mr. Barrett I have seen nothing, heard nothing. Wherever I go they play my books, with my name in big letters. *Oliver Twist* was at Baltimore when I left it last Wednesday. *Pickwick* is here, and *Dot and the Carrier* are here. *Pickwick* was at New York too when I last passed that way; so was *Our Mutual Friend;* so was *No Thoroughfare.*

We are getting now among smaller halls, but the audiences are immense. *Marigold* here last night (for the first time) bowled Philadelphia clean over. I go on to Washington to-morrow morning, and shall be half-way through my Readings on Friday, my birthday.

God bless you.

Ever affectionately,   C. D.

No. 26, Wellington Street, Strand,
London, W. C.,
Thursday, Fourth June, 1868.

MY DEAR WILKIE,—I have been to Paris. The piece is a genuine and real success. They all agree that if it could have been done at the Porte St. Martin it would have gone 200 nights. I did not see it on the first night, being far too nervous and oppressed by a terrible sense of the helplessness of the situation. Fechter, too, was lead-colored, and shaking from head to foot. So we took a ride in an open coach, and repaired at intervals to the Café Vaudeville, where Didier (the announced translator) came from act to act with his report. Joey Ladle knew nothing of his part, and made less than nothing of it; all the rest did well. Bertrand was loudly called at the end of the second act, and did his very utmost. There is no doubt whatever that it was a success from first to last. It was too late to make the change when I got to Paris, and Fechter had great faith in the retention of the scene besides, but I am quite certain that the piece would go better without Wilding's death scene. The audience are told (in the person of Vendale) that Wilding is dead, and that is quite enough. I saw our French Wilding after his decease, and could very clearly perceive that he had got mighty little out of it.

I thought it as well that they should know

about Paris at the Adelphi, so I went behind for half an hour last night.

You are getting on, I hope?

Ever affect'ly,   C. D.

Collins and Fechter, in 1869, wrote an original play called *Black and White.* It was produced at the London Adelphi in the month of March of that year, with Fechter as the Count de Layrac and Miss Carlotta Leclercq as Emily Milburn.

A. Y. R. Office,
Monday, Twenty-fifth February, 1869.

MY DEAR WILKIE,—I have read the play [*Black and White*] with great attention, and with a stage eye; and I think it will be *a great success.* It is highly interesting, admirably constructed and carried through, and very picturesque. Characters well marked and contrasted, sharp dialogue, and all good.

I am now going to make a suggestion or two.

The introduction and carrying on of that cane is so new and strong that I don't think the culminating situation of that act up to it. Have you and Fetcher ever thought of mak-

K.-

Gads Hill Place,
Higham by Rochester, Kent.

Wednesday Thirtieth November, 1869

Dear Sir

As I had (not) intended of communicating with you in reference to the early sheets of my narration (mistaken of my being perfectly unselfish) and on fast business relations in reference, I think it courteous (of) you to know that I had made a great mistake in my remembrance. Then to take a

Osgood and Co. have reminded me that
an item of agreement between us
relating so far back as April 1867, I
agreed to see the advance sheets of
my mystery story to them. The fact had
altogether passed out of my recollection.
Thanks

Faithfully yours
Charles Dickens

Messrs. Harper & Brothers.

ing the blow fall on Miss Leclercq by accident : of her being struck on the bosom, and
declaring that she will bear the mark as a
mark of glory and not of shame, because she
loves him ?

That is what *I* should do with it.

Before that situation, turn back to page 35.
Would it not be better if Maurice's " You
shall feel my cane on your back" were followed by Wolf's rejoinder (unheard by him
on going off), " You shall feel it on yours " ?

Page 49 : I would be very careful not to
have too much measuring, and in particular
not too much speaking about it. I would
express as much as possible of that in the
actor's doubtful manner and indecision—
with the fiddles and mutes, etc., in the or-
chestra.

Page 55 and 56 : I cannot understand
Fechter's gayety here. I took it for certain,
not having read to the end, that he had then
got the letter for the Provost Marshal in his
pocket and had read it. I cannot conceive
his jesting at that time under any other con-
ditions, and I think that it destroys the effect
of the letter when it does come.

11

This is all I have to say, except of praise and high hope—and it's little enough, I think.

Ever affec'ly,   C. D.

Dickens died on the 9th of June, 1870. Collins, who saw him laid by the side of Johnson and Garrick, in Westminster Abbey, rests now in Kensal Green, not far from the graves of Sydney Smith and Leigh Hunt.

Dickens's last letter to Collins, so far as is known to the executors of either man, was upon business matters, and was dated five months before Dickens's death. It is here appended.

No. 26, Wellington Street, Strand,
London, W. C.,
Thursday, Twenty-seventh January, 1870.

MY DEAR WILKIE,—At your request I can have no hesitation in stating for your satisfaction that the copyright in any of your novels, tales, and articles which have appeared in the periodicals entitled *Household Words* and *All the Year Round* was never purchased by the proprietors of those Periodicals, they having merely purchased from you the right of first publishing the same therein, and of course of always retaining them as an integral part of their stereotype plates. You have the right, hereby freely acknowledged, of disposing of and publishing the same novels, tales, and articles in any way you think proper, without interference from the proprietors of the said periodicals, their successors or assigns.

Faithfully yours always,

CHARLES DICKENS.

WILKIE COLLINS, Esquire.

No. 26, Wellington Street, Strand,
London, W. C.
Thursday, Twenty-seventh January, 1870.

MY DEAR WILKIE,—Within you will find the original draft of the formal letter you want from me, with my version of the same under my hand. My departure, even from the original excruciating phraseology, is very slight. May the Spirit of English Style be merciful to me!

I have been truly concerned to hear of your bad attack. Well, I have two hopes of it—first, that it will not last long; second, that it will leave you in a really recovered state of good health. I don't come to see you because I don't want to bother you. Perhaps you may be glad to see me by-and-bye.   Who knows?

Affectionately always,

CHARLES DICKENS.

WHO KNOWS?

INDEX.

CHARLES DICKENS'S WORKS.

HARPER'S HOUSEHOLD EDITION.

Profusely Illustrated. 8vo, Cloth.

OLIVER TWIST. $1 00.

MARTIN CHUZZLEWIT. $1 50.

THE OLD CURIOSITY SHOP. $1 25.

DAVID COPPERFIELD. $1 50.

DOMBEY AND SON. $1 50.

NICHOLAS NICKLEBY. $1 50.

THE PICKWICK PAPERS. $1 50.

BLEAK HOUSE. $1 50.

LITTLE DORRITT. $1 50.

BARNABY RUDGE. $1 50.

A TALE OF TWO CITIES. $1 00.

OUR MUTUAL FRIEND. $1 50.

CHRISTMAS STORIES. $1 50.

GREAT EXPECTATIONS. $1 50.

THE UNCOMMERCIAL TRAVELLER, ETC. $1 50.

PICTURES FROM ITALY, ETC. $1 50.

PUBLISHED BY HARPER & BROTHERS, NEW YORK.

☞ *The above works will be sent by mail, postage prepaid, to any part of the United States, Canada, or Mexico, on receipt of the price.*

WILKIE COLLINS'S WORKS.

ILLUSTRATED LIBRARY EDITION.

12mo, Cloth, $1 25 per volume.

Complete Sets, 17 vols., Cloth, $19 50; Half Calf, $49 50.

PUBLISHED BY HARPER & BROTHERS, NEW YORK.

☞ *The above works will be sent by mail, postage prepaid, to any part of the United States, Canada, or Mexico, on receipt of the price.*

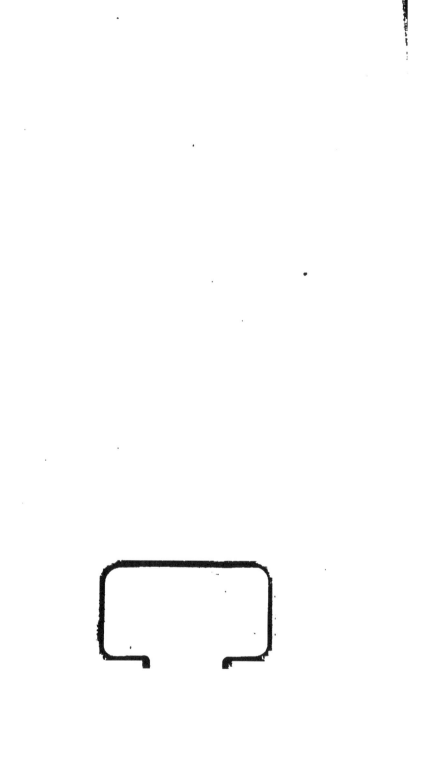

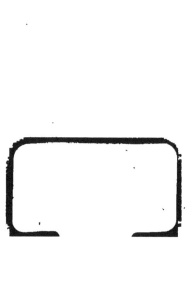

Milton Keynes UK
Ingram Content Group UK Ltd.
UKHW022104150124
436101UK00005B/121